D1736756

CONTENTS

INTRODUCTION

First of all, there is really no such thing as grilling indoors. And by the way, the biggest safety precaution of all is, don't try to use an outdoor grill anywhere indoors, including a garage or any other type of enclosed structure.

Beyond that, so-called indoor grilling is really just using alternate cooking techniques to mimic the effects of grilling.

Even if you have a high-end range with a built-in grill (and the accompanying oven hood), you can almost replicate cooking on an outdoor gas grill, but not completely. And charcoal grilling can only happen outside, and it's from charcoal that we obtain the truly high temperatures characteristic of grilling.

Every other cooking technique is at best an imitation of grilling.

Top 13 Indoor Grilling Tips for Newbies

1. Pan-Sear Your Meats Before Grilling In The Oven

One of the first things you should realize when cooking meats is how to bring out the natural flavors. The easiest way to imitate the robust flavor of outdoor grilling is by searing your meats in a pan before you place them in an oven grill.

Put a little of your favorite oil in a cast iron pan along with some seasonings. Let the pan heat, and fry the outer-layer until it's lightly charred. You'll have much more flavor than from traditional oven grilling.

2. Don't Add Salt Until Serving

Salting foods before cooking can seriously affect the texture of your dish. It can remove too much moisture from vegetables, and it can toughen the texture of red meats. You should avoid adding any salts to your meal until it's completely done.

This electric grill tip applies to seasonings as well. You're going to lose a lot of liquid content from grilling. The last thing you want is a dry chicken breast with strong flavors.

3. Add Butter And Olive Oil For Flavor

It might seem a little pointless to add oils on a steak you're cooking on an electric tabletop grill. The main point of using one is to remove all of those unhealthy fats, but certain oils really improve a dish. It's not going to seriously impact the healthy aspects of indoor grilling to add a splash of oil.

Most of the oils you add are going to be cooked away. It's really about adding complexity to your pallet. Your guests will definitely pick up on the subtle hints of olive oil, but they won't have to worry much about counting calories.

4. Cast Iron Grilling

If you're looking for a more visual appeal, then you should try using a cast iron grill pan. You can pick one up at virtually any kitchen supply store. These cast iron skillets are typically flat with lots of raised lines to create that iconic look.

Presentation is half of the process. You'll want your foods to taste great, and you'll want them to look pretty on the plate. This is one of those indoor grill tips that could get your next t-bone its own photo-shoot from the family.

5. Fat Draining Electric Tabletop Grills

This is probably the most underrated type of appliance in your kitchen. It's a lot better than most people realize. Your meats get cooked super-fast because it's pretty much pressing two hot plates together on both sides. The downside is that it can be frustrating to clean afterward.

One of the more helpful electric grill tips is to use heatproof parchment paper to cover your meat in before you cook it. This keeps your electric tabletop grill perfectly clean without having to scrub away burnt on grease.

6. Smoked Seasonings

All of the indoor grill tips in the world can't put that smokey flavor you get from charcoal, but smoked seasonings certainly can! Keep it simple. Just add a little smoked paprika to your regular seasonings for a nice kick.

A good quality chipotle marinade can really take your dish to the next level. Try to avoid adding liquid smoke to meats because it can overpower the flavor of beef.

7. Preheat The Grill

You should always preheat the electric grill you're using to a fairly hot temperature. Never put cold meat on a cold cooking surface. This is one of the professional electric grill cooking tips that a lot of people don't know about.

A faster cook time means that your foods will retain their moisture levels better than slowly heating up the cooking surface with the meat. Improper heating of the pan can also cause the meat to cook unevenly. Make sure your electric grill really sizzles when you place uncooked food on it.

8. Grilled And Steamed Veggies

Don't forget that your indoor grill is great for cooking a variety of veggies. Try wrapping your broccoli in a parchment paper the next time you grill. You can get the same tenderness that you would from steaming, but with the added bonus of a little charred flavor.

9. Try A Food Torch

You'll definitely leave an impression on your dinner guests if you pull out a food torch to top off their succulent meal. It's a really showy way to imitate the flame-broiled tastes of a propane grill. Just be sure to stay safe while you set the food on fire.

Always make sure you fully cook any meats you put on the grill. The ThermoPro Food Thermometer company makes a whole bunch of different gadgets that'll have you feeling like a culinary master. It's always better to be safe than sorry.

BREAKFAST RECIPES

Corn Cakes With Salsa And Cream Cheese

Servings: 8

Cooking Time: 8 Minutes

Ingredients:

- ½ cup Cornmeal
- ¼ cup Butter, melted
- ½ cup Salsa
- 14 ounces canned Corn, drained
- 1 cup Milk
- 6 ounces Cream Cheese
- 1 ½ cups Flour
- 6 Eggs
- ¼ cup chopped Spring Onions
- 1 tsp Baking Powder
- Salt and Pepper, to taste

Directions:

1. In a bowl, whisk together the eggs, butter, cream cheese, and milk.
2. Whisk in the cornmeal, flour, baking powder, salt, and pepper.
3. Fold in the remaining ingredients and stir well to incorporate.
4. Preheat your grill to medium.
5. When the light is on, unlock the hinge and lower to your counter.
6. Spray the griddle with a nonstick spray.
7. Ladle the batter onto the griddle (about ¼ of cup per cake).
8. When the cakes start bubbling, flip them over and cook until golden brown.
9. Serve as desired and enjoy!

Nutrition:

- InfoCalories 325 ;Total Fats 15g ;Carbs 35g ;Protein 11g ;Fiber: 3g

Grilled Ham Omelet

Servings: 2
Cooking Time: 5 Minutes

Ingredients:

- 6 Eggs
- 2 Ham Slices, chopped
- 2 tbsp chopped Herbs by choice
- ¼ tsp Onion Powder
- 1 tbsp minced Red Pepper
- ¼ tsp Garlic Powder
- Salt and Pepper, to taste

Directions:

1. Preheat your grill to 350 degrees F.
2. In the meantime, whisk the eggs in a bowl and add the rest of the ingredients to it. Stir well to combine.
3. Open the grill and unlock the hinge.
4. Coat the griddle with some cooking spray and gently pour the egg mixture onto it.
5. With a silicone spatula, mix the omelet as you would in a skillet.
6. When it reaches your desired consistency, divide among two serving plates.
7. Enjoy!

Nutrition:

- InfoCalories 271 ;Total Fats 17.5g ;Carbs 2.4g ;Protein 24g ;Fiber: 0.1g

Chocolate Chip And Blueberry Pancakes

Servings: 2

Cooking Time: 5 Minutes

Ingredients:

- 1 cup Pancake Mix
- ¼ cup Orange Juice
- 1/3 cup Fresh Blueberries
- ¼ cup Chocolate Chips
- ½ cup Water

Directions:

1. Preheat your grill to medium.
2. Meanwhile, combine the pancake mix with the orange juice and water.
3. Fold in the chocolate chips and blueberries.
4. Open the grill, unhinge, and lay the griddle onto your counter.
5. Spray with cooking spray.
6. Add about 1/6 of the batter at a time, to the griddle.
7. Cook until bubbles start forming on the surface, then flip over, and cook until the other side turns golden brown.
8. Serve and enjoy!

Nutrition:

- InfoCalories 370 ;Total Fats 9g ;Carbs 66g ;Protein 3g ;Fiber: 3g

Mexican Eggs On Haystacks

Servings: 6

Cooking Time: 12 Minutes

Ingredients:

- ½ cup Breadcrumbs
- 3 ½ cups Store-Bought Hash Browns
- 2/3 cup Sour Cream
- 2 tsp Tex Mex Seasoning
- 6 Eggs
- 1/3 cup shredded Cheddar
- Salt and Pepper, to taste

Directions:

1. Preheat your grill to medium.
2. In the meantime, squeeze the hash browns to get rid of excess water, and place in a bowl.
3. Add the breadcrumbs, cheese, half of the Tex-Mex, and season with some salt and pepper.
4. Mix with your hands to combine.
5. Open the grill, unlock the hinge for the griddle, and lay it open. Spray with cooking spray.
6. Make six patties out of the hash brown mixture and arrange onto the griddle.
7. Cook for 7 minutes, flipping once, halfway through. Tarsnsfer to six serving plates.
8. Crack the eggs open onto the griddle, season with salt and pepper, and cook until they reach your preferred consistency.
9. Top the hash browns with the egg.
10. Combine the sourcream and remaining Tex Mex and top the eggs with it.
11. Enjoy!

Nutrition:

- InfoCalories 340 ;Total Fats 21g ;Carbs 25g ;Protein 8.2g ;Fiber: 2g

Classic Bacon And Eggs Breakfast

Servings: 1
Cooking Time: 8 Minutes

Ingredients:
- 2 Eggs
- 2 Bacon Slices
- 2 Bread Slices
- Salt and Pepper, to taste

Directions:
1. Preheat your grill to 400 degrees F, and make sure that the kickstand is in position.
2. When the light goes on, add the bacon to the plate and lower the lid.
3. Let cook for 4 full minutes.
4. Open the lid and crack the eggs onto the plate. Season with salt and pepper.
5. Add the bread slices to the plate, as well.
6. Cook for 4 minutes, turning the bread and bacon (and the eggs if you desire) over ha-lfway through.
7. Transfer carefully to a plate. Enjoy!

Nutrition:
- InfoCalories 434 ;Total Fats 19.6g ;Carbs 38.8g ;Protein 25.6g ;Fiber: 6g

Quick Oat & Banana Pancakes

Servings: 4

Cooking Time: 5 Minutes

Ingredients:

- ½ cup Oats
- ¼ cup chopped Nuts by choice (Walnuts and Hazelnuts work best)
- 1 large Ripe Banana, chopped finely
- 2 cups Pancake Mix

Directions:

1. Preheat your grill to medium and unlock the hinge. Open it flat on your counter.
2. Meanwhile, prepare the pancake mix according to the instruction on the package.
3. Stir in the remaining ingredients well.
4. Spray the griddle with some cooking spray.
5. Drop about ¼ cup onto the griddle.
6. Cook for a minute or two, just until the pancake begins to puff up.
7. Flip over and cook for another minute or so – the recipe makes about 16 pancakes.
8. Serve as desired and enjoy!

Nutrition:

- InfoCalories 310 ;Total Fats 8g ;Carbs 56g ;Protein 14g ;Fiber: 8g

Sausage And Mushroom Breakfast Skewers

Servings: 4
Cooking Time: 4 Minutes

Ingredients:
- 2 Italian Sausage Links
- 4 Whole White Button Mushrooms
- 1 Red Bell Pepper
- Salt and Pepper, to taste

Directions:
1. Soak four skewers in cold water for 2-3 minutes.
2. Preheat your grill to 375 degrees F.
3. Meanwhile, cut each sausage in eight pieces.
4. Quarter the mushrooms and cut the red pepper into eight pieces.
5. Sprinkle the mushrooms and pepper generously with salt and pepper.
6. Grab the skewers and thread the ingredients – sausage, mushroom, pepper, sausage mushroom, sausage mushroom, pepper, sausage, mushroom, in that order.
7. Place onto the grill and lower the lid.
8. Cook for 4 minutes closed.
9. Serve alongside some bread and a favorite spread and enjoy.

Nutrition:
- InfoCalories 118 ;Total Fats 9.1g ;Carbs 4g ;Protein 7.3g ;Fiber: 0.6g

BREADS AND SANDWICHES

The Greatest Butter Burger Recipe

Servings: 6
Cooking Time: 11 Minutes

Ingredients:
- 2 pounds Ground Chuck Meat
- 1 ½ tsp minced Garlic
- 6 tbsp Butter
- 2 tbsp Worcestershire Sauce
- 1 tsp Salt
- ½ tsp Pepper
- 6 Hamburger Buns
- Veggie Toppings of Choice

Directions:
1. Preheat your grill to medium-high.
2. Meanwhile, place the meat, garlic, sauce, salt, and pepper, in a bowl.
3. Mix with your hands to incorporate well. Make six patties out of the mixture.
4. Into each patty, press about one tablespoon into the center.
5. Open the grill and coat with some cooking spray.
6. Arrange the patties onto the bottom plate and cook for 6 minutes.
7. Flip over and cook for 5 more minutes.
8. Serve in hamburger buns with desired veggie toppings.
9. Enjoy!

Nutrition:
- InfoCalories 595 ;Total Fats 48g ;Carbs 25g ;Protein 27g ;Fiber: 1.5g

Simple Pork Chop Sandwich

Servings: 4

Cooking Time: 7 Minutes

Ingredients:

- 4 Hamburger Buns
- 4 Cheddar Slices
- 4 boneless Pork Chop
- Salt and Pepper, to taste
- 4 tbsp Mayonnaise

Directions:

1. Preheat your grill to 375 degrees F.
2. When the green light turns on, open the grill.
3. Season the pork chops with salt and pepper and arrange onto the bottom plate.
4. Lower the lid, and cook the meat closed, for about 5-6 minutes.
5. Open the lid and place a slice of cheddar on top of each chop.
6. Cook for another minute or so, uncovered, until the cheese starts to melt.
7. Spread a tbsp of mayonnaise onto the insides of each bun.
8. Place the cheesy pork chop inside and serve.
9. Enjoy!

Nutrition:

- InfoCalories 510 ;Total Fats 30.6g ;Carbs 18.4g ;Protein 42g ;Fiber: 5g

Chicken Pesto Grilled Sandwich

Servings: 2

Cooking Time: 4 Minutes

Ingredients:

- 4 Slices of Bread
- 1 ½ cups shredded Mozzarella Cheese
- ½ cup Pesto Sauce
- 2 cups cooked and shredded Chicken Meat
- 8 Sundried Tomatoes
- 1 ½ tbsp Butter

Directions:

1. Preheat your grill to medium-high.
2. Combine the pesto and chicken in a bowl.
3. Brush the outsides of the bread with the butter.
4. Divide the pesto/chicken filling between two bread slices.
5. Top with sundried tomatoes and mozzarella cheese.
6. Open the grill and carefully transfer the loaded slices of bread onto the top bottom.
7. Top with the remaining bread slices, carefully.
8. Lower the lid, pressing gently.
9. Let the sandwiches cook for about 3-4 minutes, or until the desired doneness is reached.
10. Serve and enjoy!

Nutrition:

- InfoCalories 725 ;Total Fats 44.5g ;Carbs 32g ;Protein 51g ;Fiber: 7.5g

Fish Tacos With Slaw And Mango Salsa

Servings: 4

Cooking Time: 6 Minutes

Ingredients:

- 4 Tortillas
- 1-pound Cod
- 3 tbsp butter, melted
- ½ tsp Paprika
- ¼ tsp Garlic Onion
- 1 tsp Thyme
- ½ tsp Onion Powder
- ½ tsp Cayenne Pepper
- 1 tsp Brown Sugar
- 1 cup prepared (or store-brought) Slaw
- Salt and Pepper, to taste
- Mango Salsa:
- ¼ cup diced Red Onions
- Juice of 1 Lime
- 1 Mango, diced
- 1 Jalapeno Pepper, deseeded and minced
- 1 tbsp chopped Parlsey or Cilantro

Directions:

1. Preheat your grill to medium.
2. Brush the butter over the cod and sprinkle with the spices.
3. When ready, open the grill, and arrange the cod fillets onto the bottom plate.
4. Lower the lid and cook for about 4-5 minutes in total.
5. Transfer to a plate and cut into chunks.
6. Place all of the mango salsa ingredients in a bowl and mix to combine.
7. Assemble the tacos by adding slaw, topping with grilled cod, and adding a tablespoon or so of the mango salsa.
8. Enjoy!

Nutrition:

- InfoCalories 323 ;Total Fats 12g ;Carbs 31g ;Protein 24g ;Fiber: 3g

Buttery Pepperoni Grilled Cheese Sandwich

Servings: 2
Cooking Time: 5 Minutes

Ingredients:
- 4 slices of Bread
- 4 slices of Mozzarella Cheese
- 4 tbsp Butter
- 18 Pepperoni Slices

Directions:
1. Preheat your grill to medium-high.
2. Meanwhile, brush each slice of bread with a tablespoon of butter. It seems like too much, but the taste is just incredible.
3. Divide the mozzarella and pepperoni among the insides of two bread slices.
4. Top the sandwich with the other slices of bread, keeping the buttery side up.
5. When the green light appears, open the grill.
6. Place the sandwiches carefully onto the bottom plate.
7. Lower the lid, and gently press.
8. Allow the sandwich to cook for 4-5 minutes.
9. Open the lid, transfer to a serving plate, cut in half, and serve. Enjoy!

Nutrition:
- InfoCalories 625 ;Total Fats 46g ;Carbs 29g ;Protein 22g ;Fiber: 2g

Cheesy Buffalo Avocado Sandwich

Servings: 4

Cooking Time: 4 Minutes

Ingredients:
- 1 Avocado
- 2 Bread Slices
- 2 slices Cheddar Cheese
- 1 tbsp Butter
- Buffalo Sauce:
- 4 tbsp Hot Sauce
- 1 tbs White Vinegar
- ¼ cup Butter
- ¼ tsp Salt
- 1 tsp Cayenne Pepper
- ¼ tsp Garlic Salt

Directions:
1. Preheat your grill to 375 degrees F.
2. Meanwhile, peel the avocado, scoop out the flash, and mash it with a fork.
3. Spread the avocado onto a bread slice, and top with the cheddar cheese.
4. Spread the butter onto the outside of the other bread slice.
5. Top the sandwich with the buttery slice, with the butter-side up.
6. Grease the bottom cooking plate and place the sandwich there, with the butter-side up.
7. Lower the lid, press, and let the sandwich grill for about 4 minutes.
8. Meanwhile, whisk together all of the sauce ingredients.
9. Serve the sandwich with the Buffalo sauce and enjoy!

Nutrition:
- InfoCalories 485 ;Total Fats 24g ;Carbs 35g ;Protein 8g ;Fiber: 3g

VEGETARIAN RECIPES

Marinated Veggie Skewers

Servings: 4
Cooking Time: 10 Minutes

Ingredients:
- For Marinade:
- 2 garlic cloves, minced
- 2 teaspoons fresh basil, minced
- 2 teaspoons fresh oregano, minced
- ½ teaspoon cayenne pepper
- Sea Salt and ground black pepper, as required
- 2 tablespoons fresh lemon juice
- 2 tablespoons olive oil
- For Veggies:
- 2 large zucchinis, cut into thick slices
- 8 large button mushrooms, quartered
- 1 yellow bell pepper, seeded and cubed
- 1 red bell pepper, seeded and cubed

Directions:

1. For marinade: in a large bowl, add all the ingredients and mix until well combined.
2. Add the vegetables and toss to coat well.
3. Cover and refrigerate to marinate for at least 6-8 hours.
4. Remove the vegetables from the bowl and thread onto pre-soaked wooden skewers.
5. Place the water tray in the bottom of Power XL Smokeless Electric Grill.
6. Place about 2 cups of lukewarm water into the water tray.
7. Place the drip pan over water tray and then arrange the heating element.
8. Now, place the grilling pan over heating element.
9. Plugin the Power XL Smokeless Electric Grill and press the 'Power' button to turn it on.
10. Then press 'Fan" button.
11. Set the temperature settings according to manufacturer's directions.
12. Cover the grill with lid and let it preheat.
13. After preheating, remove the lid and grease the grilling pan.
14. Place the skewers over the grilling pan.
15. Cover with the lid and cook for about 8-10 minutes, flipping occasionally.
16. Serve hot.

Nutrition:

- Info (Per Serving):Calories 122 ;Total Fat 7.8 g ;Saturated Fat 1.2 g ;Cholesterol 0 mg ;Sodium 81 mg ;Total Carbs 12.7 g ;Fiber 3.5 g ;Sugar 6.8g ;Protein 4.3 g

Pineapple & Veggie Skewers

Servings: 6

Cooking Time: 15 Minutes

Ingredients:

- 1/3 cup olive oil
- 1½ teaspoons dried basil
- ¾ teaspoon dried oregano
- Salt and ground black pepper, as required
- 2 zucchinis, cut into 1-inch slices
- 2 yellow squash, cut into 1-inch slices
- ½ pound whole fresh mushrooms
- 1 red bell pepper, cut into chunks
- 1 red onion, cut into chunks
- 12 cherry tomatoes
- 1 fresh pineapple, cut into chunks

Directions:

1. In a bowl, add oil, herbs, salt ad black pepper and mix well.
2. Thread the veggies and pineapple onto pre-soaked wooden skewers.
3. Brush the veggiesand pineapple with oil mixture evenly.
4. Place the water tray in the bottom of Power XL Smokeless Electric Grill.
5. Place about 2 cups of lukewarm water into the water tray.
6. Place the drip pan over water tray and then arrange the heating element.
7. Now, place the grilling pan over heating element.
8. Plugin the Power XL Smokeless Electric Grill and press the 'Power' button to turn it on.
9. Then press 'Fan" button.
10. Set the temperature settings according to manufacturer's directions.
11. Cover the grill with lid and let it preheat.
12. After preheating, remove the lid and grease the grilling pan.
13. Place the skewers over the grilling pan.
14. Cover with the lid and cook for about 10-15 minutes, flipping occasionally.
15. Serve hot.

Nutrition:

- Info (Per Serving):Calories 220 ;Total Fat 11.9 g ;Saturated Fat 1.7 g ;Cholesterol 0 mg ;Sodium 47 mg ;Total Carbs 30 g ;Fiber 5 g ;Sugar 20.4 g ;Protein 4.3 g

Haloumi Kebobs

Servings: 4
Cooking Time: 5 Minutes

Ingredients:
- ½ pound Haloumi Cheese
- 4 Cremini Mushrooms, cut in half
- 1 Zucchini, cut into chunks
- ½ Bell Pepper, cut into chunks
- 2 tbsp Olive Oil
- Salt and Pepper, to taste

Directions:
1. Preheat your grill to 375 degrees F.
2. Meanwhile, soak 8 wooden skewers in water to preven burning.
3. Cut the cheese int chunks.
4. Thread the cheese and veggies onto the skewers, drizzle with the olive oil and sprinkle with salt and pepper.
5. Arrange onto the bottom plate, lower the lid, and cook closed for about 5 minutes (or more if you want it well-done).
6. Serve as desired and enjoy!

Nutrition:
- InfoCalories 220 ;Total Fats 14g ;Carbs 6g ;Protein 5g ;Fiber: 1.2g

Buttered Corn

Servings: 6
Cooking Time: 20 Minutes

Ingredients:
- 6 fresh whole corn on the cob
- ½ cup butter, melted
- Salt, as required

Directions:
1. Husk the corn and remove all the silk.
2. Brush each corn with melted butter and sprinkle with salt.
3. Place the water tray in the bottom of Power XL Smokeless Electric Grill.
4. Place about 2 cups of lukewarm water into the water tray.
5. Place the drip pan over water tray and then arrange the heating element.
6. Now, place the grilling pan over heating element.
7. Plugin the Power XL Smokeless Electric Grill and press the 'Power' button to turn it on.
8. Then press 'Fan" button.
9. Set the temperature settings according to manufacturer's directions.
10. Cover the grill with lid and let it preheat.
11. After preheating, remove the lid and grease the grilling pan.
12. Place the corn over the grilling pan.
13. Cover with the lid and cook for about 20 minutes, rotating after every 5 minutes and brushing with butter once halfway through.
14. Serve warm.

Nutrition:
- Info (Per Serving):Calories 268 ;Total Fat 17.2 g ;Saturated Fat 10 g ;Cholesterol 41 mg ;Sodium 159 mg ;Total Carbs 29 g ;Fiber 4.2 g ;Sugar 5 g ;Protein 5.2 g

Goat Cheese & Tomato Stuffed Zucchini

Servings: 8

Cooking Time: 8 Minutes

Ingredients:

- 14 ounces Goat Cheese
- 1 ½ cups Tomato Sauce
- 4 medium Zucchini

Directions:

1. Preheat your grill to medium-high.
2. Cut the zucchini in half and scoop the seeds out.
3. Coat the grill with cooking spray and add the zucchini to it.
4. Lower the lid and cook for 2 minutes.
5. Now, add half of the goat cheese first, top with tomato sauce, and place the remaining cheese on top. Place a piece of aluminum foil on top of the filling so you don't make a big mess.
6. Carefully lower the grill and cook for an additional minute.
7. Serve and enjoy!

Nutrition:

- InfoCalories 170 ;Total Fats 11g ;Carbs 8.2g ;Protein 10.5g ;Fiber: 2.3g

Vinegar Veggies

Servings: 4
Cooking Time: 10 Minutes

Ingredients:

- 3 golden beets, trimmed, peeled and sliced thinly
- 3 carrots, peeled and sliced lengthwise
- 1 cup zucchini, sliced
- 1 onion, sliced
- ½ cup yam, sliced thinly
- 2 tablespoon fresh rosemary
- 1 garlic clove, minced
- Salt and ground black pepper, as required
- 3 tablespoons vegetable oil
- 2 teaspoons balsamic vinegar

Directions:

1. Place all ingredients in a bowl and toss to coat well.
2. Refrigerate to marinate for at least 30 minutes.
3. Place the water tray in the bottom of Power XL Smokeless Electric Grill.
4. Place about 2 cups of lukewarm water into the water tray.
5. Place the drip pan over water tray and then arrange the heating element.
6. Now, place the grilling pan over heating element.
7. Plugin the Power XL Smokeless Electric Grill and press the 'Power' button to turn it on.
8. Then press 'Fan" button.
9. Set the temperature settings according to manufacturer's directions.
10. Cover the grill with lid and let it preheat.
11. After preheating, remove the lid and grease the grilling pan.
12. Place the vegetables over the grilling pan.
13. Cover with the lid and cook for about 5 minutes per side.
14. Serve hot.

Nutrition:

- Info (Per Serving):Calories 184 ;Total Fat 10.7 g ;Saturated Fat 2.2 g ;Cholesterol 0 mg ;Sodium 134 mg ;Total Carbs 21.5 g ;Fiber 4.9 g ;Sugar 10 g ;Protein 2.7 g

Stuffed Zucchini

Servings: 6
Cooking Time: 24 Minutes

Ingredients:

- 3 medium zucchinis, sliced in half lengthwise
- 1 teaspoon vegetable oil
- Salt and ground black pepper, as required
- 3 cup corn, cut off the cob
- 1 cup Parmesan cheese, shredded
- 2/3 cup sour cream
- ¼ teaspoon hot sauce
- Olive oil cooking spray

Directions:

1. Cut the ends off the zucchini and slice in half lengthwise.
2. Scoop out the pulp from each half of zucchini, leaving the shell.
3. For filling: in a large pan of boiling water, add the corn over medium heat andcook for about 5-7 minutes.
4. Drain the corn and set aside to cool.
5. In a large bowl, add corn, haf of the parmesan cheese, sour cream and hot sauce and mix well.
6. Spray the zucchini shells with cooking spray evenly.
7. Place the water tray in the bottom of Power XL Smokeless Electric Grill.
8. Place about 2 cups of lukewarm water into the water tray.
9. Place the drip pan over water tray and then arrange the heating element.
10. Now, place the grilling pan over heating element.
11. Plugin the Power XL Smokeless Electric Grill and press the 'Power' button to turn it on.
12. Then press 'Fan" button.
13. Set the temperature settings according to manufacturer's directions.
14. Cover the grill with lid and let it preheat.
15. After preheating, remove the lid and grease the grilling pan.
16. Place the zucchini halves over the grilling pan, flesh side down.
17. Cover with the lid and cook for about 8-10 minutes.
18. Remove the zucchini halves from grill.
19. Spoon filling into each zucchini half evenly and sprinkle with remaining parmesan cheese.
20. Place the zucchini halves over the grilling pan.
21. Cover with the lid and cook for about 8 minutes.
22. Serve hot.

Nutrition:

- Info (Per Serving):Calories 198 ;Total Fat 10.8 g ;Saturated Fat 6 g ;Cholesterol 21 mg ;Sodium 293 mg ;Total Carbs 19.3 g ;Fiber 3.2 g ;Sugar 4.2 g ;Protein 9.6 g

Guacamole

Servings: 4

Cooking Time: 4 Minutes

Ingredients:

- 2 ripe avocados, halved and pitted
- 2 teaspoons vegetable oil
- 3 tablespoons fresh lime juice
- 1 garlic clove, crushed
- ¼ teaspoon ground chipotle chile
- Salt, as required
- ¼ cup red onion, chopped finely
- ¼ cup fresh cilantro, chopped finely

Directions:

1. Brush the cut sides of each avocado half with oil.
2. Place the water tray in the bottom of Power XL Smokeless Electric Grill.
3. Place about 2 cups of lukewarm water into the water tray.
4. Place the drip pan over water tray and then arrange the heating element.
5. Now, place the grilling pan over heating element.
6. Plugin the Power XL Smokeless Electric Grill and press the 'Power' button to turn it on.
7. Then press 'Fan" button.
8. Set the temperature settings according to manufacturer's directions.
9. Cover the grill with lid and let it preheat.
10. After preheating, remove the lid and grease the grilling pan.
11. Place the avocado halves over the grilling pan, cut side down.
12. Cook, uncovered for about 2-4 minutes.
13. Transfer the avocados onto cutting board and let them cool slightly.
14. Remove the peel and transfer the flesh into a bowl.
15. Add the lime juice, garlic, chipotle and salt and with a fork, mash until almost smooth.
16. Stir in onion and cilantro and refrigerate, covered for about 1 hour before serving.

Nutrition:

- Info (Per Serving):Calories 230 ;Total Fat 21.9 g ;Saturated Fat 4.6g ;Cholesterol 0 mg ;Sodium 46 mg ;Total Carbs 9.7 g ;Fiber 6.9 g ;Sugar 0.8 g ;Protein 2.1 g

Caprese Eggplant Boats

Servings: 4
Cooking Time: 10 Minutes

Ingredients:
- 2 Eggplants
- 1 cup Cherry Tomatoes, halved
- 1 cup Mozzarella Balls, chopped
- 2 tbsp Olive Oil
- 4 tbsp chopped Basil Leaves
- Salt and Pepper, to taste

Directions:
1. Preheat your grill to 375 degrees F.
2. Cut the eggplants in half (no need to peel them- just wash well), drizzle with olive oil and season with salt and pepper, generously.
3. When the green light is on, open the grill and arrange the eggplant halves onto the bottom plate.
4. Lower the lid and cook for about 4-5 minutes, until well-done.
5. Transfer to a serving plate and top with cherry tomatoes, mozzarella and basil.
6. Serve and enjoy!

Nutrition:
- InfoCalories 187 ;Total Fats 11g ;Carbs 18.3g ;Protein 6.8g ;Fiber: 7.3g

Spinach And Cheese Portobellos

Servings: 3
Cooking Time: 6 Minutes

Ingredients:

- 3 Portobello Mushrooms
- 2 cups Spinach, chopped
- 1 cup shredded Cheddar Cheese
- 4 ounces Cream Cheese
- 1 tbsp Olive Oil
- 1 tsp minced Garlic
- Salt and Pepper, to taste

Directions:

1. Preheat your grill to 350 degrees F.
2. Clean the mushroom caps well, and pat dry with paper towels.
3. Remove the stems, so the fillign can fit.
4. Now, make the filling by mixing the cheeses, spinach, and garlic. Divide this mixture among the mushrooms.
5. Drizzle with olive oil.
6. When the green light is on, open the grill and add the mushrooms.
7. Arrange on top of the plate and cook with the lid off for about 5 minutes.
8. Now, lower the lid gently, but do not use pressure. Let cook for 15-20 seconds, just so the cheese melts faster.
9. Transfer to a serving plate and enjoy!

Nutrition:

- InfoCalories 210 ;Total Fats 9g ;Carbs 5g ;Protein 10g ;Fiber: 1g

Garlicky Mixed Veggies

Servings: 4
Cooking Time: 8 Minutes

Ingredients:

- 1 bunch fresh asparagus, trimmed
- 6 ounces fresh mushrooms, halved
- 6 Campari tomatoes, halved
- 1 red onion, cut into 1-inch chunks
- 3 garlic cloves, minced
- 2 tablespoons olive oil
- Salt and ground black pepper, as required

Directions:

1. In a large bowl, add all ingredients and toss to coat well.
2. Place the water tray in the bottom of Power XL Smokeless Electric Grill.
3. Place about 2 cups of lukewarm water into the water tray.
4. Place the drip pan over water tray and then arrange the heating element.
5. Now, place the grilling pan over heating element.
6. Plugin the Power XL Smokeless Electric Grill and press the 'Power' button to turn it on.
7. Then press 'Fan" button.
8. Set the temperature settings according to manufacturer's directions.
9. Cover the grill with lid and let it preheat.
10. After preheating, remove the lid and grease the grilling pan.
11. Place the vegetables over the grilling pan.
12. Cover with the lid and cook for about 8 minutes, flipping occasionally.

Nutrition:

- Info (Per Serving):Calories 137 ;Total Fat 7.7 g ;Saturated Fat 1.1 g   ;Cholesterol 0 mg   ;Sodium 54 mg ;Total Carbs 15.6 g   ;Fiber 5.6 g ;Sugar 8.9 g   ;Protein 5.8 g

APPETIZER & SIDE DISHES

Simple Mushrooms

Servings: 2
Cooking Time: 5 Minutes

Ingredients:
- 8 ounces shiitake mushrooms, stems discarded
- 1 tablespoon vegetable oil
- 1 garlic clove, minced
- Salt and ground black pepper, as required

Directions:
1. In a bowl, place all ingredients and toss to coat well.
2. Place the water tray in the bottom of Power XL Smokeless Electric Grill.
3. Place about 2 cups of lukewarm water into the water tray.
4. Place the drip pan over water tray and then arrange the heating element.
5. Now, place the grilling pan over heating element.
6. Plugin the Power XL Smokeless Electric Grill and press the 'Power' button to turn it on.
7. Then press 'Fan" button.
8. Set the temperature settings according to manufacturer's directions.
9. Cover the grill with lid and let it preheat.
10. After preheating, remove the lid and grease the grilling pan.
11. Place the mushrooms over the grilling pan.
12. Cover with the lid and cook for about 4-5 minutes, turning occasionally.
13. Serve hot.

Nutrition:
- Info (Per Serving):Calories 87 ;Total Fat 7.1 g ;Saturated Fat 1.3 g   ;Cholesterol 0 mg   ;Sodium 84 mg ;Total Carbs 4.2 g   ;Fiber 1.2 g ;Sugar 2 g   ;Protein 3.7 g

Bacon-wrapped Asparagus

Servings: 4

Cooking Time: 12 Minutes

Ingredients:

- 12 fresh asparagus spears, trimmed
- Olive oil cooking spray
- 1/8 teaspoon ground black pepper
- 6 bacon strips, halved lengthwise

Directions:

1. Spray the asparagus spears wit cooing spry evenly.
2. Wrap a bacon piece around each asparagus spear and then secure ends with toothpicks.
3. Place the water tray in the bottom of Power XL Smokeless Electric Grill.
4. Place about 2 cups of lukewarm water into the water tray.
5. Place the drip pan over water tray and then arrange the heating element.
6. Now, place the grilling pan over heating element.
7. Plugin the Power XL Smokeless Electric Grill and press the 'Power' button to turn it on.
8. Then press 'Fan" button.
9. Set the temperature settings according to manufacturer's directions.
10. Cover the grill with lid and let it preheat.
11. After preheating, remove the lid and grease the grilling pan.
12. Place the asparagus spears over the grilling pan.
13. Cover with the lid and cook for about 4-6 minutes per side.
14. Discard the toothpicks and serve warm.

Nutrition:

- Info (Per Serving):Calories 250 ;Total Fat 18.3 g ;Saturated Fat 6 g ;Cholesterol 48 mg ;Sodium 1004 mg ;Total Carbs 3.5 g ;Fiber 1.5 g ;Sugar 1.4 g ;Protein 17.7 g

Grilled Brussels Sprouts

Servings: 2

Cooking Time: 9 Minutes

Ingredients:

- 1 lb. brussels sprouts, halved
- 3 tablespoons olive oil
- ¼ cup balsamic vinegar
- 1 tablespoon honey
- 1 tablespoon mustard
- 2 teaspoons crushed red pepper flakes
- Kosher salt
- ½ cup Parmesan, grated

Directions:

1. Mix oil, vinegar, honey, mustard, red pepper flakes, and salt in a bowl.
2. Toss in brussels sprout and toss well to coat.
3. Turn the "Selector" knob to the "Grill Panini" side.
4. Preheat the bottom grill of Cuisine Griddler at 350 degrees F and the upper grill plate on medium heat.
5. Once it is preheated, open the lid and place the brussels sprouts in the Griddler.
6. Close the griddler's lid and grill the brussels sprouts for 7-9 minutes until lightly charred.
7. Garnish with parmesan.

Nutrition:

- Info (Per Serving): Calories 121 ;Total Fat 3.8 g ;Saturated Fat 0.7 g ;Cholesterol 22 mg ;Sodium 620 mg ;Total Carbs 8.3 g ;Fiber 2.4 g ;Sugar 1.2 g ;Protein 5.4 g

Garlicky Mushroom Skewers With Balsamic Vinegar

Servings: 4

Cooking Time: 4 Minutes

Ingredients:

- 2 pounds Button Mushrooms, halved
- 1 tbsp Tamari Sauce
- 2 tbsp Balsamic Vinegar
- ½ tsp Dried Thyme
- 2 large Garlic Cloves, minced
- Salt and Pepper, to taste

Directions:

1. Place the tamari, balsamic, thyme, and garlic, in a bowl.
2. Season with some salt and pepper and mix well to combine.
3. Add the mushrooms and toss to coat them well.
4. Cover the bowl and place in the fridge for about 30 minutes.
5. While the mushrooms are marinating, soak your wooden skewers in water to prevent burning.
6. Preheat your grill to 375 degrees F.
7. Thread the mushrooms onto your skewers and place on top of the bottom plate.
8. Grill for 2 minutes, then flip over, and grill for another two minutes, or until tender.
9. Serve and enjoy!

Nutrition:

- InfoCalories 62 ;Total Fats 1g ;Carbs 9g ;Protein 7g ;Fiber: 2g

Cauliflower Zucchini Skewers

Servings: 8

Cooking Time: 10 Minutes

Ingredients:

- 4 large zucchinis sliced
- 1 head cauliflower, cut into florets
- Olive oil, for drizzling
- kosher salt, to taste
- Black pepper, to taste
- 1/4 cup crumbled feta

Directions:

1. Alternately, thread the cauliflower and zucchini slices on the wooden skewers.
2. Drizzle olive oil, black pepper and salt over the skewers.
3. Turn the "Selector" knob to the "Grill Panini" side.
4. Preheat the bottom grill of Cuisine Griddler at 300 degrees F and the upper grill plate on medium heat.
5. Once it is preheated, open the lid and place the skewers in the Griddler.
6. Close the griddler's lid and grill the cauliflower skewers for 10 minutes.
7. Garnish with feta cheese.
8. Serve.

Nutrition:

- Info (Per Serving): Calories 191 ;Total Fat 12.2 g ;Saturated Fat 2.4 g ;Cholesterol 110 mg ;Sodium 276 mg ;Total Carbs 5 g ;Fiber 0.9 g ;Sugar 1.4 g ;Protein 8.8 g

Butter Glazed Green Beans

Servings: 4
Cooking Time: 5 Minutes

Ingredients:
- 1-lb. fresh green beans, trimmed
- 1/2 teaspoon Cajun seasoning
- 1 tablespoon butter, melted

Directions:
1. Toss green beans with butter and Cajun seasoning in a bowl.
2. Turn the "Selector" knob to the "Grill Panini" side.
3. Preheat the bottom grill of Cuisine Griddler at 350 degrees F and the upper grill plate on medium heat.
4. Once it is preheated, open the lid and place the green beans in the Griddler.
5. Close the griddler's lid and grill the green beans for 5 minutes.
6. Serve warm.

Nutrition:
- Info (Per Serving): Calories 304 ;Total Fat 30.6 g ;Saturated Fat 13.1 g ;Cholesterol 131 mg ;Sodium 834 mg ;Total Carbs 21.4 g ;Fiber 0.2 g ;Sugar 0.3 g ;Protein 4.6 g

Grilled Butternut Squash

Servings: 4

Cooking Time: 8 Minutes

Ingredients:
- 1 medium butternut squash, sliced
- 1 tablespoon olive oil
- 1 ½ teaspoons dried oregano
- 1 teaspoon dried thyme
- 1/2 teaspoon salt
- 1/4 teaspoon black pepper

Directions:
1. Peel and slice the squash into ½ inch thick slices.
2. Remove the center of the slices to discard the seeds.
3. Toss the squash slices with remaining ingredients in a bowl.
4. Turn the "Selector" knob to the "Grill Panini" side.
5. Preheat the bottom grill of Cuisine Griddler at 350 degrees F and the upper grill plate on medium heat.
6. Once it is preheated, open the lid and place the squash in the Griddler.
7. Close the griddler's lid and grill the squash for 8 minutes.
8. Serve warm.

Nutrition:
- Info (Per Serving): Calories 249 ;Total Fat 11.9 g ;Saturated Fat 1.7 g ;Cholesterol 78 mg ;Sodium 79 mg ;Total Carbs 41.8 g ;Fiber 1.1 g ;Sugar 20.3 g ;Protein 15 g

Zucchini Roulades

Servings: 8
Cooking Time: 12 Minutes

Ingredients:

- 4 medium zucchinis
- 1 cup part-skim ricotta cheese
- ¼ cup Parmesan cheese, grated
- 2 tablespoons fresh basil, minced
- 1 tablespoon Greek olives, chopped
- 1 tablespoon capers, drained
- 1 teaspoon lemon zest, grated
- 1 tablespoon fresh lemon juice
- Salt and ground black pepper, as required

Directions:

1. Cut each zucchini into 1/8-inch thick slices lengthwise.
2. Place the water tray in the bottom of Power XL Smokeless Electric Grill.
3. Place about 2 cups of lukewarm water into the water tray.
4. Place the drip pan over water tray and then arrange the heating element.
5. Now, place the grilling pan over heating element.
6. Plugin the Power XL Smokeless Electric Grill and press the 'Power' button to turn it on.
7. Then press 'Fan" button.
8. Set the temperature settings according to manufacturer's directions.
9. After preheating, remove the lid and grease the grilling pan.
10. Place half of the zucchini slices over the grilling pan.
11. Cover with the lid and cook for about 2-3 minutes per side.
12. Transfer the zucchini slices onto a platter.
13. Repeat with the remaining slices.
14. Meanwhile, in a small bowl, place the remaining ingredients and mix well. Set aside.
15. Place about 1 tablespoon of cheese mixture on the end of each zucchini slice.
16. Roll up and secure each with a toothpick.
17. Serve immediately.

Nutrition:

- Info (Per Serving):Calories 70 ;Total Fat 3.4 g ;Saturated Fat 1.9 g   ;Cholesterol 12 mg   ;Sodium 131 mg ;Total Carbs 5.1 g   ;Fiber 1.2 g ;Sugar 1.9 g   ;Protein 5.8 g

Jalapeño Poppers

Servings: 12
Cooking Time: 30 Minutes

Ingredients:
- 24 medium jalapeño peppers
- 1 pound uncooked chorizo pork sausage, crumbled
- 2 cups cheddar cheese, shredded
- 12 bacon strips, cut in half

Directions:
1. Cut each jalapeno in half lengthwise, about 1/8-inch deep.
2. Then remove the seeds.
3. In a bowl, place the sausage and cheese and mix well.
4. Stuff the jalapeño peppers with cheese mixture and then wrap each with a piece of bacon.
5. With toothpicks, secure each jalapeño pepper.
6. Place the water tray in the bottom of Power XL Smokeless Electric Grill.
7. Place about 2 cups of lukewarm water into the water tray.
8. Place the drip pan over water tray and then, arrange the heating element.
9. Now, place the grilling pan over heating element.
10. Plugin the Power XL Smokeless Electric Grill and press the 'Power' button to turn it on.
11. Then press 'Fan" button.
12. Set the temperature settings according to manufacturer's directions.
13. Cover the grill with lid and let it preheat.
14. After preheating, remove the lid and grease the grilling pan.
15. Place the jalapeño peppers over the grilling pan.
16. Cover with the lid and cook for about 35-40 minutes, flipping once halfway through.
17. Discard the toothpicks and serve warm.

Nutrition:
- Info (Per Serving):Calories 373 ;Total Fat 29.5 g ;Saturated Fat 11.4 g ;Cholesterol 83 mg ;Sodium 1800 mg ;Total Carbs 2.7 g ;Fiber 1.1 g ;Sugar 1 g ;Protein 23.2 g

Grilled Zucchini

Servings: 4
Cooking Time: 6 Minutes

Ingredients:
- 1-pound Zucchini
- 1 tbsp Lemon Juice
- 2 Garlic Cloves, minced
- 2 tbsp Olive Oil
- 1 tsp Italian Seasoning
- Salt and Pepper, to taste

Directions:
1. Trim and peel the zucchini. Cut into thick slices and place in a bowl.
2. Add all of the remaining ingredients and mix well so that the zucchini slices are completely coated.
3. Cover the bowl and place in the fridge for about one hour.
4. Menawhile, preheat your HB grill to 375 degrees F.
5. When the green light turns on, open the grill and place the zucchini slices onto the bottom plate.
6. Cook with the lid off, for three minutes. Flip over and cook for another three minutes.
7. Serve as desired and enjoy!

Nutrition:
- InfoCalories 76 ;Total Fats 7g ;Carbs 1g ;Protein 0g ;Fiber: 0g

Veggie Burger

Servings: 5
Cooking Time: 5 Minutes

Ingredients:
- 1 cup cooked brown rice
- 1 cup raw walnuts, finely chopped
- 1/2 tablespoons avocado oil
- 1/2 medium white onion, diced
- 1 tablespoon chili powder
- 1 tablespoon cumin powder
- 1 tablespoon smoked paprika
- 1/2 teaspoons sea salt
- 1/2 teaspoons black pepper
- 1 tablespoon coconut sugar
- 1 ½ cups cooked black beans, drained
- 1/3 cup panko bread crumbs
- 4 tablespoons BBQ sauce

Directions:
1. Add brown rice, walnuts, and all the veggies burger ingredients to a food processor.
2. Blend this mixture for 3 minutes then transfer to a bowl.
3. Make 5 patties out of this vegetable beans mixture.
4. Turn the "Selector" knob to the "Grill Panini" side.
5. Preheat the bottom grill of Cuisine Griddler at 350 degrees F and the upper grill plate on medium heat.
6. Once it is preheated, open the lid and place the veggie burgers in the Griddler.
7. Close the griddler's lid and grill the burgers for 5 minutes.
8. Serve warm.

Nutrition:
- Info (Per Serving): Calories 213 ;Total Fat 14 g ;Saturated Fat 8 g ;Cholesterol 81 mg ;Sodium 162 mg ;Total Carbs 23 g ;Fiber 0.7 g ;Sugar 19 g ;Protein 12 g

POULTRY RECIPES

Grilled Chicken Skewers

Servings: 4
Cooking Time: 5 Minutes

Ingredients:
- 1/4 cup fresh lime juice
- 2 garlic cloves, sliced
- 1 chipotle chile in adobo, chopped
- Kosher salt and black pepper, to taste
- 2 boneless chicken breasts, cut into chunks

Directions:
1. Mix chicken cubes with black pepper, salt, chile, garlic and lime juice in a bowl.
2. Thread the chicken cubes on the wooden skewers.
3. Turn the "Selector" knob to the "Grill Panini" side.
4. Preheat the bottom grill of Cuisine Griddler at 350 degrees F and the upper grill plate on medium heat.
5. Once it is preheated, open the lid and place the skewers in the Griddler.
6. Close the griddler's lid and grill the skewers for 5 minutes.
7. Serve warm.

Nutrition:
- Info (Per Serving): Calories 440 ;Total Fat 7.9 g ;Saturated Fat 1.8 g ;Cholesterol 5 mg ;Sodium 581 mg ;Total Carbs 21.8 g ;Sugar 7.1 g ;Fiber 2.6 g ;Protein 37.2 g

Meatballs Kabobs

Servings: 4

Cooking Time: 14 Minutes

Ingredients:

- 1 yellow onion, chopped roughly
- ½ cup lemongrass, chopped roughly
- 2 garlic cloves, chopped roughly
- 1½ pounds lean ground turkey
- 1 teaspoon sesame oil
- ½ tablespoons low-sodium soy sauce
- 1 tablespoon arrowroot starch
- 1/8 teaspoons powdered stevia
- Salt and ground black pepper, as required

Directions:

1. In a food processor, add the onion, lemongrass and garlic and pulse until chopped finely.
2. Transfer the onion mixture into a large bowl.
3. Add the remaining ingredients and mix until well combined.
4. Make 12 equal sized balls from meat mixture.
5. Thread the balls onto the presoaked wooden skewers.
6. Place the water tray in the bottom of Power XL Smokeless Electric Grill.
7. Place about 2 cups of lukewarm water into the water tray.
8. Place the drip pan over water tray and then arrange the heating element.
9. Now, place the grilling pan over heating element.
10. Plugin the Power XL Smokeless Electric Grill and press the 'Power' button to turn it on.
11. Then press 'Fan" button.
12. Set the temperature settings according to manufacturer's directions.
13. Cover the grill with lid and let it preheat.
14. After preheating, remove the lid and grease the grilling pan.
15. Place the skewers over the grilling pan.
16. Cover with the lid and cook for about 6-7 minutes per side.
17. Serve hot.

Nutrition:

- Info (Per Serving):Calories 276 ;Total Fat 13.4 g ;Saturated Fat 4 g ;Cholesterol 122 mg ;Sodium 280 mg ;Total Carbs 5.6 g ;Fiber 0.6 g ;Sugar 1.3 g ;Protein 34.2 g

Ketchup Glaze Chicken Thighs

Servings: 12

Cooking Time: 16 Minutes

Ingredients:

- ½ cup packed brown sugar
- 1/3 cup ketchup
- 1/3 cup low-sodium soy sauce
- 3 tablespoons sherry
- 1½ teaspoons fresh ginger root, minced
- 1½ teaspoons garlic, minced
- 12 (6-ounce) boneless, skinless chicken thighs

Directions:

1. In a small bowl, place all ingredients except for chicken thighs and mix well.
2. Transfer about 1 1/3 cups for marinade in another bowl and refrigerate.
3. In a zip lock bag, add the remaining marinade and chicken thighs.
4. Seal the bag and shake to coat well.
5. Refrigerate overnight.
6. Remove the chicken thighs from bag and discard the marinade.
7. Place the water tray in the bottom of Power XL Smokeless Electric Grill.
8. Place about 2 cups of lukewarm water into the water tray.
9. Place the drip pan over water tray and then arrange the heating element.
10. Now, place the grilling pan over heating element.
11. Plugin the Power XL Smokeless Electric Grill and press the 'Power' button to turn it on.
12. Then press 'Fan" button.
13. Set the temperature settings according to manufacturer's directions.
14. Cover the grill with lid and let it preheat.
15. After preheating, remove the lid and grease the grilling pan.
16. Place the chicken thighs over the grilling pan.
17. Cover with the lid and cook for about 6-8 minutes per side.
18. In the last 5 minutes of cooking, baste the chicken thighs with reserved marinade.
19. Serve hot.

Nutrition:

- Info (Per Serving):Calories 359 ;Total Fat 12.6 g ;Saturated Fat 3.6 g ;Cholesterol 151 mg ;Sodium 614 mg ;Total Carbs 8.3 g ;Fiber 0 g ;Sugar 7.6 g ;Protein 49.8 g

Marinated Chicken Breasts

Servings: 4
Cooking Time: 16 Minutes

Ingredients:

- ¼ cup extra-virgin olive oil
- 2 tablespoons fresh lemon juice
- 2 tablespoons maple syrup
- 1 garlic clove, minced
- Salt and ground black pepper, as required
- 4 (6-ounce) boneless, skinless chicken breasts

Directions:

1. For marinade: in a large bowl, add oil, lemon juice, maple syrup, garlic, salt and black pepper and beat until well combined.
2. In a large resealable plastic bag, place the chicken and marinade.
3. Seal the bag and shake to coat well.
4. Refrigerate overnight.
5. Place the water tray in the bottom of Power XL Smokeless Electric Grill.
6. Place about 2 cups of lukewarm water into the water tray.
7. Place the drip pan over water tray and then arrange the heating element.
8. Now, place the grilling pan over heating element.
9. Plugin the Power XL Smokeless Electric Grill and press the 'Power' button to turn it on.
10. Then press 'Fan" button.
11. Set the temperature settings according to manufacturer's directions.
12. Cover the grill with lid and let it preheat.
13. After preheating, remove the lid and grease the grilling pan.
14. Place the chicken breasts over the grilling pan.
15. Cover with the lid and cook for about 5-8 minutes per side.
16. Serve hot.

Nutrition:

- Info (Per Serving):Calories 460 ;Total Fat 25.3 g ;Saturated Fat 5.3 g ;Cholesterol 151 mg ;Sodium 188 mg ;Total Carbs 7.1 g ;Fiber 0.1 g ;Sugar 6.1 g ;Protein 49.3 g

Chicken Drumsticks

Servings: 5
Cooking Time: 40 Minutes

Ingredients:

- 2 tablespoons avocado oil
- 1 tablespoon fresh lime juice
- 1 teaspoon red chili powder
- 1 teaspoon garlic powder
- Salt, as required
- 5 (8-ounce) chicken drumsticks

Directions:

1. In a mixing bowl, mix avocado oil, lime juice, chili powder and garlic powder and mix well.
2. Add the chicken drumsticks and coat with the marinade generously.
3. Cover the bowl and refrigerate to marinate for about 30-60 minutes.
4. Place the water tray in the bottom of Power XL Smokeless Electric Grill.
5. Place about 2 cups of lukewarm water into the water tray.
6. Place the drip pan over water tray and then arrange the heating element.
7. Now, place the grilling pan over heating element.
8. Plugin the Power XL Smokeless Electric Grill and press the 'Power' button to turn it on.
9. Then press 'Fan" button.
10. Set the temperature settings according to manufacturer's directions.
11. Cover the grill with lid and let it preheat.
12. After preheating, remove the lid and grease the grilling pan.
13. Place the chicken drumsticks over the grilling pan.
14. Cover with the lid and cook for about 30-40 minutes, flipping after every 5 minutes.
15. Serve hot.

Nutrition:

- Info (Per Serving):Calories 395 ;Total Fat 13.8 g ;Saturated Fat 3.6 g ;Cholesterol 200 mg ;Sodium 218 mg ;Total Carbs 1 g ;Fiber 0.5 g ;Sugar 0.2 g ;Protein 62.6 g

Thyme Duck Breasts

Servings: 2

Cooking Time: 16 Minutes

Ingredients:

- 2 shallots, sliced thinly
- 1 tablespoon fresh ginger, minced
- 2 tablespoons fresh thyme, chopped
- Salt and ground black pepper, as required
- 2 duck breasts

Directions:

1. In a large bowl, place the shallots, ginger, thyme, salt, and black pepper, and mix well.
2. Add the duck breasts and coat with marinade evenly.
3. Refrigerate to marinate for about 2-12 hours.
4. Place the water tray in the bottom of Power XL Smokeless Electric Grill.
5. Place about 2 cups of lukewarm water into the water tray.
6. Place the drip pan over water tray and then arrange the heating element.
7. Now, place the grilling pan over heating element.
8. Plugin the Power XL Smokeless Electric Grill and press the 'Power' button to turn it on.
9. Then press 'Fan" button.
10. Set the temperature settings according to manufacturer's directions.
11. Cover the grill with lid and let it preheat.
12. After preheating, remove the lid and grease the grilling pan, skin-side down.
13. Place the duck breast over the grilling pan.
14. Cover with the lid and cook for about 6-8 minutes per side.
15. Serve hot.

Nutrition:

- Info (Per Serving):Calories 337 ;Total Fat 10.1 g ;Saturated Fat 0 g ;Cholesterol 0 mg ;Sodium 80 mg ;Total Carbs 3.4 g ;Fiber 0 g ;Sugar 0.1 g ;Protein 55.5 g

Peach Glazed Chicken Breasts

Servings: 4
Cooking Time: 10 Minutes

Ingredients:

- For Chicken:
- ¼ teaspoon ground cinnamon
- ¼ teaspoon ground nutmeg
- ¼ teaspoon ground cloves
- Salt, as required
- 4 (5-6-ounce) boneless skinless chicken breasts
- For Glaze:
- 1 peach, peeled and pitted
- 1 chipotle in adobo sauce
- 2 tablespoons fresh lemon juice

Directions:

1. In a bowl, place spices and salt and mix well.
2. Rub the chicken breasts with the spice mixture evenly.
3. For glaze: in a food processor, place peach, chipotle and lemon juice and pulse until pureed.
4. Transfer into a bowl and set aside.
5. Place the water tray in the bottom of Power XL Smokeless Electric Grill.
6. Place about 2 cups of lukewarm water into the water tray.
7. Place the drip pan over water tray and then arrange the heating element.
8. Now, place the grilling pan over heating element.
9. Plugin the Power XL Smokeless Electric Grill and press the 'Power' button to turn it on.
10. Then press 'Fan" button.
11. Set the temperature settings according to manufacturer's directions.
12. Cover the grill with lid and let it preheat.
13. After preheating, remove the lid and grease the grilling pan.
14. Place the chicken breasts over the grilling pan.
15. Cover with the lid and cook for about 8-10 minutes per side, brushing with the glaze after every 2 minutes.
16. Serve hot.

Nutrition:

- Info (Per Serving):Calories 287 ;Total Fat 10.7 g ;Saturated Fat 3 g ;Cholesterol 126 mg ;Sodium 163 mg ;Total Carbs 3.9 g ;Fiber 0.8 g ;Sugar 3.7 g ;Protein 41.5 g

Marinated Chicken Kabobs

Servings: 4
Cooking Time: 15 Minutes

Ingredients:
- 1/3 cup extra-virgin olive oil, divided
- 2 garlic cloves, minced
- 1 tablespoon fresh rosemary, minced
- 1 tablespoon fresh oregano, minced
- 1 teaspoon fresh lemon zest, grated
- ½ teaspoon red chili flakes, crushed
- 1 pound boneless, skinless chicken breast, cut into ¾-inch cubes
- 1¾ cups green seedless grapes, rinsed
- ½ teaspoon salt
- 1 tablespoon fresh lemon juice

Directions:

1. In small bowl, add ¼ cup of oil, garlic, fresh herbs, lemon zest and chili flakes and beat until well combined.
2. Thread the chicken cubes and grapes onto 12 metal skewers.
3. In a large baking dish, arrange the skewers.
4. Place the marinade and mix well.
5. Refrigerate to marinate for about 4-24 hours.
6. Place the water tray in the bottom of Power XL Smokeless Electric Grill.
7. Place about 2 cups of lukewarm water into the water tray.
8. Place the drip pan over water tray and then arrange the heating element.
9. Now, place the grilling pan over heating element.
10. Plugin the Power XL Smokeless Electric Grill and press the 'Power' button to turn it on.
11. Then press 'Fan" button.
12. Set the temperature settings according to manufacturer's directions.
13. Cover the grill with lid and let it preheat.
14. After preheating, remove the lid and grease the grilling pan.
15. Place the chicken skewers over the grilling pan.
16. Cover with the lid and cook for about 3-5 minutes per side or until chicken is done completely.
17. Remove from the grill and transfer the skewers onto a serving platter.
18. Drizzle with lemon juice and remaining oil and serve.

Nutrition:

- Info (Per Serving):Calories 310 ;Total Fat 20.1 g ;Saturated Fat 2.6 g ;Cholesterol 73 mg ;Sodium 351 mg ;Total Carbs 8.8 g ;Fiber 1.3 g ;Sugar 6.7 g ;Protein 24.6 g

Glazed Chicken Drumsticks

Servings: 12
Cooking Time: 25 Minutes

Ingredients:

- 1 (10-ounce) jar red jalapeño pepper jelly
- ¼ cup fresh lime juice
- 12 (6-ounce) chicken drumsticks
- Salt and ground black pepper, as required

Directions:

1. In a small saucepan, add jelly and lime juice over medium heat and cook for about 3-5 minutes or until melted.
2. Remove from the heat and set aside.
3. Sprinkle the chicken drumsticks with salt and black pepper.
4. Place the water tray in the bottom of Power XL Smokeless Electric Grill.
5. Place about 2 cups of lukewarm water into the water tray.
6. Place the drip pan over water tray and then arrange the heating element.
7. Now, place the grilling pan over heating element.
8. Plugin the Power XL Smokeless Electric Grill and press the 'Power' button to turn it on.
9. Then press 'Fan" button.
10. Set the temperature settings according to manufacturer's directions.
11. Cover the grill with lid and let it preheat.
12. After preheating, remove the lid and grease the grilling pan.
13. Place the chicken drumsticks over the grilling pan.
14. Cover with the lid and cook for about 15-20 minutes, flipping occasionally.
15. In the last 5 minutes of cooking, baste the chicken thighs with jelly mixture.
16. Serve hot.

Nutrition:

- Info (Per Serving):Calories 359 ;Total Fat 9.7 g ;Saturated Fat 2.6 g ;Cholesterol 150 mg ;Sodium 155 mg ;Total Carbs 17.1 g ;Fiber 0 g ;Sugar 11.4 g ;Protein 46.8 g

Grilled Duck Breasts

Servings: 4
Cooking Time: 6 Minutes

Ingredients:

- 1/4 cup olive oil
- 1 tablespoon dried oregano
- 2 pounds duck breasts
- 3 large garlic cloves, grated
- 2 lemons
- Kosher salt and black pepper, to taste

Directions:

1. Rub the duck breast with black pepper, salt, lemon juice, garlic, oregano and olive oil.
2. Place the duck breasts in a plate, cover and marinate for 30 minutes.
3. Turn the "Selector" knob to the "Grill Panini" side.
4. Preheat the bottom grill of Cuisine Griddler at 350 degrees F and the upper grill plate on medium heat.
5. Once it is preheated, open the lid and place the duck breasts in the Griddler.
6. Close the griddler's lid and grill the duck for 6 minutes.
7. Serve warm.

Nutrition:

- Info (Per Serving): Calories 301 ;Total Fat 15.8 g ;Saturated Fat 2.7 g ;Cholesterol 75 mg ;Sodium 189 mg ;Total Carbs 31.7 g ;Fiber 0.3 g ;Sugar 0.1 g ;Protein 28.2 g

Teriyaki Chicken Thighs

Servings: 4
Cooking Time: 7 Minutes

Ingredients:
- 4 Chicken Thighs
- ½ cup Brown Sugar
- ½ cup Teriyaki Sauce
- 2 tbsp Rice Vinegar
- 1 thumb-sized piece of Ginger, minced
- ¼ cup Water
- 2 tsp minced Garlic
- 1 tbsp Cornstarch

Directions:
1. Place the sugar, teriyaki sauce, vinegar, ginger, water, and garlic, in a bowl.
2. Mix to combine well.
3. Transfer half of the mixture to a saucepan and set aside.
4. Add the chicken thighs to the bowl, and coat well.
5. Cover the bowl with wrap, and place in the fridge. Let sit for one hour.
6. Preheat your grill to medium.
7. In the meantime, place the saucepan over medium heat and add the cornstarch. Cook until thickened. Remove from heat and set aside.
8. Arrange the thighs onto the preheated bottom and close the lid.
9. Cook for 5 minutes, then open, brush the thickened sauce over, and cover again.
10. Cook for additional minute or two.
11. Serve and enjoy!

Nutrition:
- InfoCalories 321 ;Total Fats 11g ;Carbs 28g ;Protein 31g ;Fiber: 1g

FISH & SEAFOOD RECIPES

Grilled Garlic Scallops

Servings: 4
Cooking Time: 4 Minutes

Ingredients:
- 1/4 cup olive oil
- Juice of 1 lemon
- 3 garlic cloves minced
- 1 tablespoon Italian seasoning
- Salt and black pepper, to taste
- 1-pound scallops

Directions:
1. Mix Italian seasoning, black pepper, salt, garlic cloves, lemon juice and olive oil in a bowl.
2. Toss in scallops, mix gently, cover and refrigerate for 30 minutes.
3. Turn the "Selector" knob to the "Griddle" side.
4. Preheat the bottom grill of Cuisine Griddler at 350 degrees F.
5. Once it is preheated, open the lid and place the scallops in the Griddler.
6. Grill the scallop for 2 minutes flip and grill for 2 minutes.
7. Serve warm.

Nutrition:
- Info (Per Serving): Calories 351 ;Total Fat 4 g ;Saturated Fat 6.3 g ;Cholesterol 360 mg ;Sodium 236 mg ;Total Carbs 19.1 g ;Sugar 0.3 g ;Fiber 0.1 g ;Protein 36 g

Tuna Steak With Avocado & Mango Salsa

Servings: 2

Cooking Time: 8 Minutes

Ingredients:

- 2 Tuna Steaks
- 1 ½ tbsp Olive Oil
- 1 tsp Paprika
- 2 tbsp Coconut Sugar
- 1 tsp Onion Powder
- ¼ tsp Pepper
- ½ tsp Salt
- 2/3 tsp Cumin
- Salsa:
- 1 Avocado, pitted and diced
- 1 Mango, diced
- 1 tbsp Olive Oil
- 1 tsp Honey
- ½ Red Onion, diced
- 2 tbsp Lime Juice
- Pinch of Salt

Directions:

1. Preheat your grill to 350-375 degrees F.
2. Place the olive oil and spices in a small bowl and rub the tuna steaks with the mixture.
3. Place on top of the bottom plate and cook for 4 minutes.
4. Flip the steaks over and cook for another 4 minutes.
5. Meanwhile, prepare the salsa by placing all of the salsa ingredients in a bowl, and mixing well to combine.
6. Transfer the grilled tuna steaks to two serving plates and divide the avocado and mango salsa among them.
7. Enjoy!

Nutrition:

- InfoCalories 280 ;Total Fats 26g ;Carbs 12g ;Protein 24g ;Fiber: 2g

The Easiest Pesto Shrimp

Servings: 2

Cooking Time: 5 Minutes

Ingredients:

- 1-pound Shrimp, tails and shells discarded
- ½ cup Pesto Sauce

Directions:

1. Place the cleaned shrimp in a bowl and add the pesto sauce to it.
2. Mix gently with your hands, until each shrimp is coated with the sauce. Let sit for about 15 minutes.
3. In the meantime, preheat your grill to 350 degrees F.
4. Open the grill and arrange the shrimp onto the bottom plate.
5. Cook with the lid off for about 2-3 minutes. Flip over and cook for an additional 2 minutes.
6. Serve as desired and enjoy!

Nutrition:

- InfoCalories 470 ;Total Fats 28.5g ;Carbs 3g ;Protein 50g ;Fiber: 0g

Lemon Pepper Salmon With Cherry Tomatoes And Asparagus

Servings: 4

Cooking Time: 5 Minutes

Ingredients:

- 4 Salmon Fillets
- 8 Cherry Tomatoes
- 12 Asparagus Spears
- 2 tbsp Olive Oil
- ½ tsp Garlic Powder
- 1 tsp Lemon Pepper
- ½ tsp Onion Powder
- Salt, to taste

Directions:

1. Preheat your grill to 375 degrees F and cut the tomatoes in half.
2. Brush the salmon, tomatoes, and sparagus with olive oil, and then sprinkle with the spices.
3. Arrange the salmon fillets, cherry tomatoes, and asparagus spears, onto the bottom plate.
4. Gently, lower the lid, and cook the fish and veggies for about 5-6 minutes, or until you reach your desired doneness (check at the 5th minute).
5. Serve and enjoy!

Nutrition:

- InfoCalories 240 ;Total Fats 14g ;Carbs 3.5g ;Protein 24g ;Fiber: 1.4g

Lemon-garlic Salmon

Servings: 4

Cooking Time: 7 Minutes

Ingredients:

- 2 garlic cloves, minced
- 2 teaspoons lemon zest, grated
- 1/2 teaspoon salt
- 1/2 teaspoon fresh rosemary, minced
- 1/2 teaspoon black pepper
- 4 salmon fillets (6 oz.)

Directions:

1. Mix garlic with lemon zest, salt, rosemary and black pepper in a bowl
2. Leave this spice mixture for 15 minutes then rub it over the salmon with this mixture.
3. Turn the "Selector" knob to the "Grill Panini" side.
4. Preheat the bottom grill of Cuisine Griddler at 350 degrees F and the upper grill plate on medium heat.
5. Once it is preheated, open the lid and place the salmon in the Griddler.
6. Close the griddler's lid and grill the salmon for 7 minutes.
7. Serve warm.

Nutrition:

- Info (Per Serving): Calories 246 ;Total Fat 7.4 g ;Saturated Fat 4.6 g ;Cholesterol 105 mg ;Sodium 353 mg ;Total Carbs 19.4 g ;Sugar 6.5 g ;Fiber 2.7 g ;Protein 37.2 g

Ginger Salmon

Servings: 3

Cooking Time: 8 Minutes

Ingredients:
- Sauce:
- ¼ tablespoons rice vinegar
- 1 teaspoons sugar
- 1/8 teaspoon salt
- ¼ tablespoon lime zest, grated
- 1/8 cup lime juice
- ½ tablespoon olive oil
- 1/8 teaspoon ground coriander
- 1/8 teaspoon ground black pepper
- 1/8 cup cilantro, chopped
- ¼ tablespoon onion, chopped
- ½ teaspoon ginger root, minced
- 1 garlic clove, minced
- 1 small cucumber, peeled, chopped
- Salmon:
- 2 tablespoons gingerroot, minced
- ¼ tablespoon lime juice
- ¼ tablespoon olive oil
- Salt, to taste
- Black pepper, to taste
- 3 (6 oz.) salmon fillets

Directions:

1. Start by blending the cucumber with all the sauce ingredients in a blender until smooth.
2. Season and rub the salmon fillets with ginger, oil, salt, black pepper, lime juice.
3. Turn the "Selector" knob to the "Grill Panini" side.
4. Preheat the bottom grill of Cuisine Griddler at 350 degrees F and the upper grill plate on medium heat.
5. Once it is preheated, open the lid and place the salmon fillets in the Griddler.
6. Close the griddler's lid and grill the salmon fillets for 8 minutes.
7. Serve warm with cucumber sauce.

Nutrition:

- Info (Per Serving): Calories 457 ;Total Fat 19.1 g ;Saturated Fat 11 g ;Cholesterol 262 mg ;Sodium 557 mg ;Total Carbs 18.9 g ;Sugar 1.2 g ;Fiber 1.7 g ;Protein 32.5 g

Simple Mahi-mahi

Servings: 4
Cooking Time: 10 Minutes

Ingredients:

- 4 (6-ounce) mahi-mahi fillets
- 2 tablespoons olive oil
- Salt and ground black pepper, as required

Directions:

1. Coat fish fillets with olive oil and season with salt and black pepper evenly.
2. Place the water tray in the bottom of Power XL Smokeless Electric Grill.
3. Place about 2 cups of lukewarm water into the water tray.
4. Place the drip pan over water tray and then arrange the heating element.
5. Now, place the grilling pan over heating element.
6. Plugin the Power XL Smokeless Electric Grill and press the 'Power' button to turn it on.
7. Then press 'Fan" button.
8. Set the temperature settings according to manufacturer's directions.
9. Cover the grill with lid and let it preheat.
10. After preheating, remove the lid and grease the grilling pan.
11. Place the fish fillets over the grilling pan.
12. Cover with the lid and cook for about 5 minutes per side.
13. Serve hot.

Nutrition:

- Info (Per Serving):Calories 195 ;Total Fat 7 g ;Saturated Fat 1 g   ;Cholesterol 60 mg   ;Sodium 182 mg ;Total Carbs 0 g   ;Fiber 0 g ;Sugar 0 g   ;Protein 31.6 g

Lemony Salmon

Servings: 4

Cooking Time: 14 Minutes

Ingredients:

- 2 garlic cloves, minced
- 1 tablespoon fresh lemon zest, grated
- 2 tablespoons butter, melted
- 2 tablespoons fresh lemon juice
- Salt and ground black pepper, as required
- 4 (6-ounce) boneless, skinless salmon fillets

Directions:

1. In a bowl, place all ingredients (except salmon fillets) and mix well.
2. Add the salmon fillets and coat with garlic mixture generously.
3. Place the water tray in the bottom of Power XL Smokeless Electric Grill.
4. Place about 2 cups of lukewarm water into the water tray.
5. Place the drip pan over water tray and then arrange the heating element.
6. Now, place the grilling pan over heating element.
7. Plugin the Power XL Smokeless Electric Grill and press the 'Power' button to turn it on.
8. Then press 'Fan" button.
9. Set the temperature settings according to manufacturer's directions.
10. Cover the grill with lid and let it preheat.
11. After preheating, remove the lid and grease the grilling pan.
12. Place the salmon fillets over the grilling pan.
13. Cover with the lid and cook for about 6-7 minutes per side.
14. Serve immediately.

Nutrition:

- Info (Per Serving):Calories 281 ;Total Fat 16.3 g ;Saturated Fat 5.2 g ;Cholesterol 90 mg ;Sodium 157 mg ;Total Carbs 1 g ;Fiber 0.2 g ;Sugar 0.3 g ;Protein 33.3 g

Grilled Scallops

Servings: 4
Cooking Time: 6 Minutes

Ingredients:
- 1-pound Jumbo Scallops
- 1 ½ tbsp Olive Oil
- ½ tsp Garlic Powder
- Salt and Pepper, to taste
- Dressing:
- 1 tbsp chopped Parsley
- 3 tbsp Lemon Juice
- ½ tsp Lemon Zest
- 2 tbsp Olive Oil
- Salt and Pepper, to taste

Directions:
1. Preheat your grill to medium-high.
2. Brush the scallops with olive oi, and sprinkle with salt, pepper, and garlic powder.
3. Arrange onto the bottom plate and cook for about 3 minutes, with the lid off.
4. Flip over, and grill for an additional two or three minutes.
5. Meanwhile, make the dressing by combining all of the ingredients in a small bowl.
6. Transfer the grilled scallops to a serving plate and drizzle the dressing over.
7. Enjoy!

Nutrition:
- InfoCalories 102 ;Total Fats 5g ;Carbs 3g ;Protein 9.5g ;Fiber: 1g

Blackened Salmon

Servings: 2

Cooking Time: 6 Minutes

Ingredients:
- 1 lb. salmon fillets
- 3 tablespoons butter, melted
- 1 tablespoon lemon pepper
- 1 teaspoon seasoned salt
- 1½ tablespoon smoked paprika
- 1 teaspoon cayenne pepper
- ¾ teaspoon onion salt
- ½ teaspoon dry basil
- ½ teaspoon ground white pepper
- ½ teaspoon ground black pepper
- ¼ teaspoon dry oregano
- ¼ teaspoon ancho chili powder

Directions:
1. Liberally season the salmon fillets with butter and other ingredients.
2. Turn the "Selector" knob to the "Grill Panini" side.
3. Preheat the bottom grill of Cuisine Griddler at 350 degrees F and the upper grill plate on medium heat.
4. Once it is preheated, open the lid and place the salmon fillets in the Griddler.
5. Close the griddler's lid and grill the fish fillets for 6 minutes.
6. Serve warm.

Nutrition:
- Info (Per Serving): Calories 378 ;Total Fat 7 g ;Saturated Fat 8.1 g ;Cholesterol 230 mg ;Sodium 316 mg ;Total Carbs 16.2 g ;Sugar 0.2 g ;Fiber 0.3 g ;Protein 26 g

Barbecue Squid

Servings: 4
Cooking Time: 3 Minutes

Ingredients:

- 1 ½ pounds skinless squid tubes, sliced
- ⅓ cup red bell pepper, chopped
- 13 fresh red Thai chiles, stemmed
- 6 garlic cloves, minced
- 3 shallots, chopped
- 1 (1-inch) piece fresh ginger, chopped
- 6 tablespoons sugar
- 2 tablespoons soy sauce
- 1 ½ teaspoons black pepper
- ¼ teaspoon salt

Directions:

1. Blend bell pepper, red chilies, shallots, sugar, soy sauce, black pepper and salt in a blender.
2. Transfer this marinade to a Ziplock bag and ad squid tubes.
3. Seal the bag and refrigerate for 1 hour for marination.
4. Turn the "Selector" knob to the "Grill Panini" side.
5. Preheat the bottom grill of Cuisine Griddler at 350 degrees F and the upper grill plate on medium heat.
6. Once it is preheated, open the lid and place the squid chunks in the Griddler.
7. Close the griddler's lid and grill the squid for 2-3 minutes.
8. Serve warm.

Nutrition:

- Info (Per Serving): Calories 248 ;Total Fat 15.7 g ;Saturated Fat 2.7 g ;Cholesterol 75 mg ;Sodium 94 mg ;Total Carbs 31.4 g ;Fiber 0.4 g ;Sugar 3.1 g ;Protein 24.9 g

BEEF, PORK & LAMB RECIPES

Hawaian Kebobs

Servings: 4
Cooking Time: 6 Minutes

Ingredients:
- ½ cup Orange Juice
- 1 tbsp minced Garlic
- 1/3 cup Brown Sugar
- ½ tbs minced Ginger
- ½ cup Soy Sauce
- 1-pound Top Sirloin
- 1-pound Pineapple, fresh
- 2 Bell Peppers
- ½ Red Onion

Directions:
1. Place the first 5 ingredients in a medium bowl. Whisk to combine well.
2. Cut the steak into pieces and add to the bowl.
3. Stir well to coat, cover with plastic wrap, and place in the fridge for at least 60 minutes.
4. Meanwhile, cut the red onion, pineapple, and bell pepper, into chunks.
5. If using wooden skewers, soak them in cold water.
6. Preheat your grill to medium-high.
7. Thread the steak, pineapple, onion, and bell peppers onto the skewers.
8. Open the grill and arrange the skewers onto the bottom plate.
9. Cover, and let cook for 6 minutes.
10. Serve and enjoy!

Nutrition:
- InfoCalories 460 ;Total Fats 13g ;Carbs 51g ;Protein 33g ;Fiber: 0.7g

Greek Souzoukaklia

Servings: 4

Cooking Time: 14 Minutes

Ingredients:

- 1 ½ pounds ground beef
- 1 onion, chopped
- ⅜ cup raisins, chopped
- 1 ½ teaspoons parsley, chopped
- ½ teaspoon cayenne pepper
- ½ teaspoon ground cinnamon
- ½ teaspoon ground coriander
- 1 pinch ground nutmeg
- ½ teaspoon white sugar
- Salt and black pepper to taste
- 1 tablespoon vegetable oil

Directions:

1. Mix ground beef with onion, raisins, and rest of the ingredients in a bowl.
2. Take a handful of this mixture and wrap it around each skewer to make a sausage.
3. Turn the "Selector" knob to the "Grill Panini" side.
4. Preheat the bottom grill of Cuisine Griddler at 350 degrees F and the upper grill plate on medium heat.
5. Once it is preheated, open the lid and place the skewers in the Griddler.
6. Close the griddler's lid and grill the skewers for 15 minutes.
7. Enjoy.

Nutrition:

- Info (Per Serving): Calories 361 ;Total Fat 16.3 g ;Saturated Fat 4.9 g ;Cholesterol 114 mg ;Sodium 515 mg ;Total Carbs 19.3 g ;Fiber 0.1 g ;Sugar 18.2 g ;Protein 33.3 g

Lamb Steak

Servings: 6

Cooking Time: 4 Minutes

Ingredients:

- 2 garlic cloves, minced
- 2 tablespoons olive oil
- 2 teaspoons dried oregano, crushed
- 2 tablespoons sumac
- 2 teaspoons sweet paprika
- 12 lamb cutlets, trimmed

Directions:

1. In a bowl mix together all ingredients except for lamb cutlets.
2. Add the cutlets and coat with garlic mixture evenly.
3. Set aside for at least 10 minutes.
4. Place the water tray in the bottom of Power XL Smokeless Electric Grill.
5. Place about 2 cups of lukewarm water into the water tray.
6. Place the drip pan over water tray and then arrange the heating element.
7. Now, place the grilling pan over heating element.
8. Plugin the Power XL Smokeless Electric Grill and press the 'Power' button to turn it on.
9. Then press 'Fan" button.
10. Set the temperature settings according to manufacturer's directions.
11. Cover the grill with lid and let it preheat.
12. After preheating, remove the lid and grease the grilling pan.
13. Place the cutlets over the grilling pan.
14. Cover with the lid and cook for about 2 minutes from both sides or until desired doneness.
15. Serve hot.

Nutrition:

- Info (Per Serving):Calories 343 ;Total Fat 16.6 g ;Saturated Fat 4.9 g ;Cholesterol 144 mg ;Sodium 122 mg ;Total Carbs 1 g ;Fiber 0.5 g ;Sugar 0.1 g ;Protein 45.2 g

Garlicy Lamb Chops

Servings: 4
Cooking Time: 6 Minutes

Ingredients:

- 1 tablespoon fresh ginger, grated
- 4 garlic cloves, chopped roughly
- 1 teaspoon ground cumin
- ½ teaspoon red chili powder
- Salt and ground black pepper, as required
- 1 tablespoon olive oil
- 1 tablespoon fresh lemon juice
- 8 lamb chops, trimmed

Directions:

1. In a bowl, mix together all ingredients except for chops.
2. With a hand blender, blend until a smooth mixture forms.
3. Add the chops and coat with mixture generously.
4. Refrigerate to marinate for overnight.
5. Place the water tray in the bottom of Power XL Smokeless Electric Grill.
6. Place about 2 cups of lukewarm water into the water tray.
7. Place the drip pan over water tray and then arrange the heating element.
8. Now, place the grilling pan over heating element.
9. Plugin the Power XL Smokeless Electric Grill and press the 'Power' button to turn it on.
10. Then press 'Fan" button.
11. Set the temperature settings according to manufacturer's directions.
12. Cover the grill with lid and let it preheat.
13. After preheating, remove the lid and grease the grilling pan.
14. Place the lamb chops over the grilling pan.
15. Cover with the lid and cook for about 3 minutes per side.
16. Serve hot.

Nutrition:

- Info (Per Serving):Calories 465 ;Total Fat 20.4 g ;Saturated Fat 6.5 g ;Cholesterol 204 mg ;Sodium 178 mg ;Total Carbs 2.4 g ;Fiber 0.4 g ;Sugar 0.2 g ;Protein 64.2 g

Margarita Beef Skewers

Servings: 6
Cooking Time: 10 Minutes

Ingredients:

- 1 cup margarita mix
- ½ teaspoon salt
- 1 tablespoon white sugar
- 2 garlic cloves, minced
- ¼ cup vegetable oil
- 1-pound top sirloin steak, cubed
- 16 mushrooms, stems trimmed
- 1 onion, cut into chunks
- 1 large red bell pepper, diced

Directions:

1. Mix margarita, salt, white sugar, garlic, vegetable, sirloin steak, mushrooms, onion, and red bell pepper on a bowl.
2. Cover and refrigerate the beef mixture for 1 hour for marination.
3. Thread the beef, mushrooms, onion and bell pepper, alternately on the wooden.
4. Turn the "Selector" knob to the "Grill Panini" side.
5. Preheat the bottom grill of Cuisine Griddler at 350 degrees F and the upper grill plate on medium heat.
6. Once it is preheated, open the lid and place the skewers in the Griddler.
7. Close the griddler's lid and grill the skewers for 10 minutes.
8. Serve warm.

Nutrition:

- Info (Per Serving): Calories 405 ;Total Fat 22.7 g ;Saturated Fat 6.1 g ;Cholesterol 4 mg ;Sodium 227 mg ;Total Carbs 26.1 g ;Fiber 1.4 g ;Sugar 0.9 g ;Protein 45.2 g

Garlicky Marinated Steak

Servings: 1

Cooking Time: 8 Minutes

Ingredients:

- 4 Steaks (about 1 - 1 ½ pounds)
- 3 tbsp minced Garlic
- ¼ cup Soy Sauce
- 2 tbsp Honey
- ¼ cup Balsamic Vinegar
- 2 tbsp Worcesteshire Sauce
- ½ tsp Onion Powder
- Salt and Pepper, to taste

Directions:

1. Whisk together the garlic, sauces, and spices, in a bowl.
2. Add the steaks to it and make sure to coat them well.
3. Cover with plastic foil and refrigerate for about an hour.
4. Preheat your grill to high.
5. Open and add your steaks to the bottom plate.
6. Lower the lid and cook for about 4 minutes, or until the meat reaches the internal temperature that you prefer.
7. Serve as desired and let sit for a couple of minutes before enjoying!

Nutrition:

- InfoCalories 435 ;Total Fats 24g ;Carbs 19g ;Protein 37g ;Fiber: 1g

Teriyaki Beef Skewers

Servings: 6

Cooking Time: 6 Minutes

Ingredients:

- ¾ cup brown sugar
- ¼ cup soy sauce
- 1/8 cup pineapple juice
- 1/8 cup water
- 2 tablespoons vegetable oil
- 1 garlic clove, chopped
- 2 pounds boneless round steak, sliced

Directions:

1. Mix brown sugar, soy sauce, pineapple juice, water, vegetable oi, garlic cloves and steak slices in a bowl.
2. Cover and refrigerate the steaks for 24 hours for marination.
3. Thread the marinated beef on the wooden skewers.
4. Turn the "Selector" knob to the "Grill Panini" side.
5. Preheat the bottom grill of Cuisine Griddler at 350 degrees F and the upper grill plate on medium heat.
6. Once it is preheated, open the lid and place the skewers in the Griddler.
7. Close the griddler's lid and grill the skewers for 6 minutes.
8. Serve warm.

Nutrition:

- Info (Per Serving): Calories 380 ;Total Fat 20 g ;Saturated Fat 5 g ;Cholesterol 151 mg ;Sodium 686 mg ;Total Carbs 33 g ;Fiber 1 g ;Sugar 1.2 g ;Protein 21 g

Grilled Lamb With Herbes De Provence

Servings: 6

Cooking Time: 18 Minutes

Ingredients:

- 1 rib (3 ounces-1-inch-thick) lamb chops
- 1/4 cups olive oil
- 2 lemons, juiced
- Salt and black pepper, to taste
- 3 tablespoons Herbes de Provence

Directions:

1. Rub the lamb chops with lemon juice, olive oil, black pepper, salt and Herbes de Provence.
2. Cover and marinate the chops for 1 hour in the refrigerator.
3. Turn the "Selector" knob to the "Grill Panini" side.
4. Preheat the bottom grill of Cuisine Griddler at 350 degrees F and the upper grill plate on medium heat.
5. Once it is preheated, open the lid and place half of the chops in the Griddler.
6. Close the griddler's lid and grill the chops for 9 minutes.
7. Transfer the grilled chops to a plate and grill the remaining chops in the same manner.
8. Serve warm.

Nutrition:

- Info (Per Serving): Calories 308 ;Total Fat 20.5 g ;Saturated Fat 3 g ;Cholesterol 42 mg ;Sodium 688 mg ;Total Carbs 40.3 g ;Sugar 1.4 g ;Fiber 4.3 g ;Protein 49 g

Lamb Kabobs

Servings: 6

Cooking Time: 10 Minutes

Ingredients:

- 1 large pineapple, cubed into 1½-inch size, divided
- 1 (½-inch) piece fresh ginger, chopped
- 2 garlic cloves, chopped
- Salt, as required
- 16-24-ounce lamb shoulder steak, trimmed and cubed into 1½-inch size
- Fresh mint leaves from a bunch
- Ground cinnamon, as required

Directions:

1. In a food processor, add about 1½ cups of pineapple, ginger, garlic and salt and pulse until smooth.
2. Transfer the mixture into a large bowl.
3. Add the chops and coat with mixture generously.
4. Refrigerate to marinate for about 1-2 hours.
5. Remove from the refrigerator.
6. Thread lamb cubes, remaining pineapple and mint leaves onto pre-soaked wooden skewers.
7. Place the water tray in the bottom of Power XL Smokeless Electric Grill.
8. Place about 2 cups of lukewarm water into the water tray.
9. Place the drip pan over water tray and then arrange the heating element.
10. Now, place the grilling pan over heating element.
11. Plugin the Power XL Smokeless Electric Grill and press the 'Power' button to turn it on.
12. Then press 'Fan" button.
13. Set the temperature settings according to manufacturer's directions.
14. Cover the grill with lid and let it preheat.
15. After preheating, remove the lid and grease the grilling pan.
16. Place the skewers over the grilling pan.
17. Cover with the lid and cook for about 10 minutes, turning occasionally.

Nutrition:

- Info (Per Serving):Calories 288 ;Total Fat 8.5 g ;Saturated Fat 3 g ;Cholesterol 102 mg ;Sodium 115 mg ;Total Carbs 20.2 g ;Fiber 2.1 g ;Sugar 14.9 g ;Protein 32.7 g

Rosemary Lamb Chops

Servings: 2
Cooking Time: 10 Minutes

Ingredients:

- 1 tablespoon olive oil
- 1 tablespoon fresh lemon juice
- 1 tablespoon fresh rosemary, chopped
- ½ teaspoon garlic, minced
- Salt and ground black pepper, as required
- 2 (8-ounce) (½-inch-thick) lamb shoulder blade chops

Directions:

1. In a bowl, place all ingredients and beat until well combined.
2. Place the chops and oat with the mixture well.
3. Seal the bag and shake vigorously to coat evenly.
4. Place the water tray in the bottom of Power XL Smokeless Electric Grill.
5. Place about 2 cups of lukewarm water into the water tray.
6. Place the drip pan over water tray and then arrange the heating element.
7. Now, place the grilling pan over heating element.
8. Plugin the Power XL Smokeless Electric Grill and press the 'Power' button to turn it on.
9. Then press 'Fan" button.
10. Set the temperature settings according to manufacturer's directions.
11. Cover the grill with lid and let it preheat.
12. After preheating, remove the lid and grease the grilling pan.
13. Place the lamb chops over the grilling pan.
14. Cover with the lid and cook for about 4-5 minutes per side.
15. Serve hot.

Nutrition:

- Info (Per Serving):Calories 410 ;Total Fat 25.4 g ;Saturated Fat 7.2 g ;Cholesterol 151 mg ;Sodium 241 mg ;Total Carbs 1.5 g ;Fiber 0.7 g ;Sugar 0.2 g ;Protein 44.3 g

Pork Burnt Ends

Servings: 1
Cooking Time: 6 Minutes

Ingredients:

- 1-pound Pork Shoulder
- 2 tbsp Favorite Rub Spice
- 2 tbsp Honey
- 1 ½ tbsp Barbecue Sauce

Directions:

1. Start by chopping the pork into cubes.
2. Place the meat in a bowl and add the spice, honey, and barbecue sauce.
3. With your hands, mix wel, making sure that each meat cube gets a little bit of honey, sauce, and spices.
4. Preheat your grill to 375 degrees F.
5. Arange the pork onto the bottom plate and lower the lid.
6. Cook for about 6 minutes.
7. Check the meat – if it is not too burnt for your taste, cook for an additional minute.
8. Serve as desired.
9. Enjoy!

Nutrition:

- InfoCalories 399 ;Total Fats 27g ;Carbs 10.8g ;Protein 27g ;Fiber: 0g

SNACK & DESSERT RECIPES

Pumpkin Cream Cheese Pancakes

Servings: 2
Cooking Time: 4 Minutes

Ingredients:
- 1 egg, beaten
- ½ cup Mozzarella cheese, shredded
- 1½ tablespoon sugar-free pumpkin puree
- 2 teaspoons heavy cream
- 1 teaspoon cream cheese, softened
- 1 tablespoon all-purpose flour
- 1 tablespoon Sugar
- ½ teaspoon pumpkin pie spice
- ½ teaspoon baking powder
- 1 teaspoon vanilla extract

Directions:
1. Turn the "Selector" knob to the "Griddle" side.
2. Preheat the bottom plate of the Cuisine GR Griddler at 350 degrees F.
3. In a medium bowl, put all ingredients and with a fork, mix until well combined.
4. Pour ½ of the mixture into preheated Griddler and cook for about 2 minutes per side.
5. Cook more pancakes using the remaining batter.
6. Serve warm.

Nutrition:
- Info (Per Serving): Calories 110 ;Total Fat 7.8 g ;Saturated Fat 3.1 g ;Cholesterol 94 mg ;Sodium 82 mg ;Total Carbs 21.3 g ;Fiber 0.8g ;Sugar 1 g ;Protein 5.2 g

Cheddar Cheese Pancakes

Servings: 2

Cooking Time: 5 Minutes

Ingredients:

- 1 egg, beaten
- ½ cup Cheddar cheese, shredded
- Pinch of salt

Directions:

1. Turn the "Selector" knob to the "Griddle" side.
2. Preheat the bottom plate of the Cuisine GR Griddler at 350 degrees F.
3. Place about 1/8 cup of cheese in the bottom of the Griddler and top with half of the beaten egg.
4. Now, place 1/8 cup of cheese on top and cook for about 5 minutes.
5. Repeat with the remaining cheese and egg.
6. Serve warm.

Nutrition:

- Info (Per Serving): Calories 145 ;Total Fat 11.6 g ;Saturated Fat 6.6 g ;Cholesterol 112 mg ;Sodium 284 g ;Total Carbs 30.5 g ;Fiber 0 g ;Sugar 0.3 g ;Protein 9.8 g

Cinnamon Grilled Peaches

Servings: 4
Cooking Time: 2 Minutes

Ingredients:
- 1/4 cup salted butter
- 1 tablespoon 1 teaspoon granulated sugar
- 1/4 teaspoon cinnamon
- 4 ripe peaches, pitted and sliced

Directions:
1. Mix sugar with butter and cinnamon in a bowl until smooth.
2. Turn the "Selector" knob to the "Grill Panini" side.
3. Preheat the bottom grill of Cuisine Griddler at 350 degrees F and the upper grill plate on medium heat.
4. Once it is preheated, open the lid and place the peach slices in the Griddler.
5. Close the griddler's lid and grill the peaches for 2 minutes.
6. Drizzle cinnamon butter on top and serve.

Nutrition:
- Info (Per Serving): Calories 401 ;Total Fat 8.9 g ;Saturated Fat 4.5 g ;Cholesterol 57 mg ;Sodium 340 mg ;Total Carbs 54.7 g ;Fiber 1.2 g ;Sugar 1.3 g ;Protein 5.3 g

Grilled Tomatoes With Garlic & Parmesan

Servings: 8

Cooking Time: 6 Minutes

Ingredients:

- ½ cup grated Parmesan Cheese
- 8 small Tomatoes, halved
- 1 tsp Garlic Powder
- 2 tbsp Olive Oil
- ¼ tsp Onion Powder
- Salt and Pepper, to taste

Directions:

1. Preheat your grill to 350 degrees F.
2. Combine the oil, garlic powder, onion powder, and salt and pepper, in a bowl.
3. Brush the tomatoes with this mixture.
4. Open the grill and arrange the tomatoes onto the plate.
5. Cook for 3 minutes, then flip over and cook for 2 more minutes.
6. Top with the parmesan cheese and cook for an additional minute.
7. Serve and enjoy!

Nutrition:

- InfoCalories 78 ;Total Fats 5.6g ;Carbs 4.5g ;Protein 3.4g ;Fiber: 1g

Veggie Sliders

Servings: 10
Cooking Time: 7 Minutes

Ingredients:
- ½ Red Onion, diced
- ¾ cup cooked Quinoa
- 15 ounces canned Kidney
- ½ cup Walnuts, crushed or ground
- 1 shake Worcestershire Sauce
- 1 tbsp Chili Powder
- Salt and Pepper, to taste

Directions:
1. Preheat your grill to 350-375 degrees F.
2. Dump all of the ingredients in a bowl and mix well with your hands to incorporate the mixture.
3. Make about 10 small patties with your hands.
4. When ready, open the grill and coat with cooking spray.
5. Arrange the patties on top of the bottom plate.
6. Lower the lid and cook closed for about 6-7 minutes.
7. Serve on top of a lettuce leaf. Enjoy!

Nutrition:
- InfoCalories 89 ;Total Fats 4.2g ;Carbs 9g ;Protein 4g ;Fiber: 3g

Blueberry Cream Cheese Pancakes

Servings: 2
Cooking Time: 4 Minutes

Ingredients:

- 1 egg, beaten
- 1/3 cup Mozzarella cheese, shredded
- 1 teaspoon cream cheese, softened
- 1 teaspoon all-purpose flour
- ¼ teaspoon baking powder
- ¾ teaspoon powdered sugar
- ¼ teaspoon ground cinnamon
- ¼ teaspoon vanilla extract
- Pinch of salt
- 1 tablespoon fresh blueberries

Directions:

1. Turn the "Selector" knob to the "Griddle" side.
2. Preheat the bottom plate of the Cuisine GR Griddler at 350 degrees F.
3. In a bowl, place all ingredients except for blueberries and beat until well combined.
4. Fold in the blueberries.
5. Pour 1/2 of the mixture into preheated Griddler and cook for about 2 minutes per side.
6. Cook more pancakes using the remaining batter.
7. Serve warm.

Nutrition:

- Info (Per Serving): Calories 90 ;Total Fat 5 g ;Saturated Fat 2.7 g ;Cholesterol 97 mg ;Sodium 161 mg ;Total Carbs 25.7 g ;Fiber 2.8 g ;Sugar 1.2 g ;Protein 5.7 g

Grilled Watermelon & Cream

Servings: 8
Cooking Time: 4 Minutes

Ingredients:

- 1 medium Watermelon
- 3 cups Whipped Cream
- 2 tbsp chopped Mint

Directions:

1. Preheat your grill to medium high.
2. Peel the melon and cut into wedges. Discard seeds if there are any.
3. Open the grill and arrange the wedges on top of the bottom plate.
4. Lower te lid and cook for 3-4 minutes.
5. Open and transfer to a cutting board.
6. Cut into smaller chunks and let cool.
7. Divide among 8 serving glasses.
8. Top with whipped cream and mint leaves.
9. Enjoy!

Nutrition:

- InfoCalories 323 ;Total Fats 17.3g ;Carbs 44g ;Protein 4.4g ;Fiber: 2.2g

Almond Butter Pancakes

Servings: 2

Cooking Time: 4 Minutes

Ingredients:
- 1 large egg, beaten
- 1/3 cup Mozzarella cheese, shredded
- 1 tablespoon sugar
- 2 tablespoons almond butter
- 1 teaspoon vanilla extract

Directions:
1. Turn the "Selector" knob to the "Griddle" side.
2. Preheat the bottom plate of the Cuisine GR Griddler at 350 degrees F.
3. In a medium bowl, put all ingredients and with a fork, mix until well combined.
4. Pour ¼ of the mixture into preheated Griddler and cook for about 2 minutes per side.
5. Cook for pancakes using the remaining batter.
6. Serve warm.

Nutrition:
- Info (Per Serving): Calories 253 ;Total Fat 12.3 g ;Saturated Fat 2 g ;Cholesterol 96 mg ;Sodium 65 mg ;Total Carbs 13.6 g ;Fiber 1.6 g ;Sugar 1.2 g ;Protein 7.9 g

Cinnamon Sugar Grilled Apricots

Servings: 4

Cooking Time: 6 Minutes

Ingredients:

- 6 smallish Apricots
- 1 tbsp Butter, melted
- 3 tbsp Brown Sugar
- ½ tbsp Cinnamon

Directions:

1. Preheat your grill to 350 degrees F.
2. Cut the apricots in half and discard the seeds.
3. When ready, open the grill and coat with cooking spray.
4. Arrange the apricots and cook for 3 minutes.
5. Flip over and cook for 3 minutes more.
6. Meanwhile, whisk together the butter, sugar, and cinnamon.
7. Transfer the grilled apricots to a serving plate.
8. Drizzle the sauce over.
9. Enjoy!

Nutrition:

- InfoCalories 92 ;Total Fats 2g ;Carbs 17g ;Protein 1g ;Fiber: 1g

Red Velvet Pancakes

Servings: 2
Cooking Time: 4 Minutes

Ingredients:

- 2 tablespoons cacao powder
- 2 tablespoons Sugar
- 1 egg, beaten
- 2 drops super red food coloring
- ¼ teaspoon baking powder
- 1 tablespoon heavy whipping cream

Directions:

1. Turn the "Selector" knob to the "Griddle" side.
2. Preheat the bottom plate of the Cuisine GR Griddler at 350 degrees F.
3. In a medium bowl, put all ingredients and with a fork, mix until well combined.
4. Pour ½ of the mixture into preheated Griddler and cook for about 2 minutes per side.
5. Cook more pancakes using the remaining batter.
6. Serve warm.

Nutrition:

- Info (Per Serving): Calories 370 ;Total Fat 6 g ;Saturated Fat 3 g ;Cholesterol 92 mg ;Sodium 34 mg ;Total Carbs 33.2 g ;Fiber 1.5 g ;Sugar 0.2 g ;Protein 3.9 g

Grilled Pineapple With Coconut Sauce

Servings: 4

Cooking Time: 8 Minutes

Ingredients:

- 1 large Pineapple
- 1 ½ tsp Cornstarch
- 2 tbsp Coconut Rum
- 1 tbsp Butter
- 1 tbsp Cream of Coconut

Directions:

1. Preheat your grill to medium high.
2. In the meantime, prepare the pineapple. Peel and slice into the size of your preference.
3. Thread the pineapple slices onto soaked skewers and open the grill.
4. Arrange on top of the bottom plate and grill for about 4 minutes per side.
5. In the meantime, whisk together the remaining ingredients in a saucepan.
6. Place over medium heat and cook until slightly thickened.
7. Serve the pineapple alongside the sauce.
8. Enjoy!

Nutrition:

- InfoCalories 235 ;Total Fats 10g ;Carbs 34g ;Protein 2g ;Fiber: 3g

OTHER FAVORITE RECIPES

Turkey Burgers

Servings: 4
Cooking Time: 12 Minutes

Ingredients:
- Olive oil cooking spray
- 12 ounces lean ground turkey
- ½ of apple, peeled, cored and grated
- ½ of red bell pepper, seeded and chopped finely
- ¼ cup red onion, minced
- 2 small garlic cloves, minced
- 1 tablespoon fresh ginger, minced
- 2½ tablespoons fresh cilantro, chopped
- 2 tablespoons curry paste
- 1 teaspoon ground cumin
- 1 teaspoon olive oil

Directions:

1. In a large bowl, add all the ingredients except for oil and mix until well combined.
2. Make 4 equal-sized burgers from mixture.
3. Brush the burgers with olive oil evenly.
4. Place the water tray in the bottom of Power XL Smokeless Electric Grill.
5. Place about 2 cups of lukewarm water into the water tray.
6. Place the drip pan over water tray and then arrange the heating element.
7. Now, place the grilling pan over heating element.
8. Plugin the Power XL Smokeless Electric Grill and press the 'Power' button to turn it on.
9. Then press 'Fan" button.
10. Set the temperature settings according to manufacturer's directions.
11. Cover the grill with lid and let it preheat.
12. After preheating, remove the lid and grease the grilling pan.
13. Place the steak over the grilling pan.
14. Cover with the lid and cook for about 5-6 minutes per side.
15. Serve hot.

Nutrition:

- Info (Per Serving):Calories 258 ;Total Fat 15.2 g ;Saturated Fat 1.8 g ;Cholesterol 87 mg ;Sodium 94 mg ;Total Carbs 9.5 g ;Fiber 1.3 g ;Sugar 4 g ;Protein 24.3 g

Chicken Caesar Salad

Servings: 4
Cooking Time: 6 Minutes

Ingredients:

- 4 Chicken Breasts, boneless and skinless
- 1 Lettuce Head
- 1/3 cup Olive Oil
- ½ tsp Dijon Mustard
- 1 tsp Lemon Juice
- ½ cup grated Parmesan Cheese
- ½ tsp Anchovy Paste
- 1 tsp Red Wine Vinegar
- 1 tsp Worcestershire Sauce
- 1 cup Croutons
- 1 tsp Honey
- Salt and Pepper, to taste

Directions:

1. Preheat your grill to medium-high heat.
2. When the green light turns on, open the grill and coat with cooking spray.
3. Season the chicken with salt and pepper and place onto the bottom plate.
4. Lower the lid and cook the chicken for 6 full minutes.
5. Transfer to a cutting board and cut into strips.
6. Chop the lettuce head and place in a bowl. Add the chicken and croutons to the bowl.
7. In a smaller bowl, whisk together the remaining ingredients and drizzle the salad with the mixture.
8. Serve and enjoy!

Nutrition:

- InfoCalories 540 ;Total Fats 35g ;Carbs 15g ;Protein 45g ;Fiber: 4g

Vegan Scrambled Eggs

Servings: 4

Cooking Time: 8 Minutes

Ingredients:
- 1 package medium tofu, crumbled
- ¼ cup nutritional yeast
- 2 teaspoons garlic powder
- ½ teaspoons turmeric
- 1 teaspoon black salt
- ½ teaspoons black pepper
- 1 cup chicken broth

Directions:
1. Blend yeast, garlic powder, turmeric, black pepper, salt, broth in a blender.
2. Pour this mixture into a bowl and stir in crumbled tofu, then mix well.
3. Turn the "Selector" knob to the "Grill Panini" side.
4. Open the top lid of the Cuisine Griddler and set the flat plate sides up.
5. Preheat the bottom plate of Cuisine Griddler at 350 degrees F and the upper plate on medium heat.
6. Once it is preheated, add the tofu mixture to both plates.
7. Stir and cook the tofu mixture for 8 minutes until set.
8. Serve warm.

Nutrition:
- Info (Per Serving): Calories 73 ;Total Fat 2.3g ;Saturated Fat 0.5g ;Cholesterol 0mg ;Sodium 783mg ;Total ;arbs 6.7g ;Fiber 3.1g ;Sugars 0.7g ;Protein 8.7g

Rib Eye Steak Salad

Servings: 4

Cooking Time: 5 Minutes

Ingredients:

- 1 ½ pounds Rib Eye Steaks
- ¼ cup Fish Sauce
- ½ cup Mint Leaves
- 4 tbsp Lime Juice
- ½ cup Coriander Leaves
- 1 Lettuce Head
- 1 cup halved Cherry Tomatoes
- Salt and Pepper, to taste

Directions:

1. Preheat your grill to 375 degrees F. Spray with cooking spray.
2. Season the steak with salt and pepper and cut into strips.
3. When ready, arrange the steak onto the bottom plate.
4. Lower the lid and cook for 4-5 minutes, depending on the doneness you wish to achieve. Transfer to a plate.
5. Chop the lettuce and add to a bowl.
6. Add the rest of the ingredients and toss well to combine and coat.
7. Top the salad with the grilled steak.
8. Serve and enjoy!

Nutrition:

- InfoCalories 350 ;Total Fats 30g ;Carbs 10g ;Protein 31g ;Fiber: 1g

Stuffed Burgers

Servings: 10
Cooking Time: 20 Minutes

Ingredients:
- For Filling:
- 2 cups cooked ham, chopped
- 2 cups fresh mushrooms, chopped
- 2 cups onion, chopped
- 3 cups cheddar cheese, shredded
- For Patties:
- 5 pounds lean ground beef
- 1/3 cup Worcestershire sauce
- 2 teaspoons hickory seasoning
- Salt and ground black pepper, as required

Directions:
1. For filling: in a bowl, mix together all ingredients. Set aside.
2. For patties: in another large bowl, add all ingredients and mix until well combined.
3. Divide beef mixture into 20 equal portions. Make equal sized patties from each portion.
4. Place 10 patties onto a smooth surface. Place cheese mixture over each patty evenly.
5. Cover with remaining patties, by pressing the edges to secure the filling.
6. Place the water tray in the bottom of Power XL Smokeless Electric Grill.
7. Place about 2 cups of lukewarm water into the water tray.
8. Place the drip pan over water tray and then arrange the heating element.
9. Now, place the grilling pan over heating element.
10. Plugin the Power XL Smokeless Electric Grill and press the 'Power' button to turn it on.
11. Then press 'Fan" button.
12. Set the temperature settings according to manufacturer's directions.
13. Cover the grill with lid and let it preheat.
14. After preheating, remove the lid and grease the grilling pan.
15. Place the burgers over the grilling pan.
16. Cover with the lid and cook for about 8-10 minutes per side.
17. Serve hot.

Nutrition:
- Info (Per Serving):Calories 623 ;Total Fat 27.7 g ;Saturated Fat 13.3 g ;Cholesterol 254 mg ;Sodium 865 mg ;Total Carbs 5.9 g ;Fiber 1 g ;Sugar 3.1 g ;Protein 82.4 g

Quinoa Burgers

Servings: 6
Cooking Time: 10 Minutes

Ingredients:
- For Burgers:
- 1 tablespoon extra-virgin olive oil
- ½ of red onion, chopped
- 1 garlic clove, minced
- 1 cup fresh kale, tough ribs removed
- 1 cup carrots, peeled and chopped roughly
- 1/3 cup fresh parsley
- 15 ounces cooked cannellini beans, drained and rinsed
- 1 cup cooked quinoa
- 1 cup gluten-free oats
- For Seasoning Mixture:
- ½ cup barbecue sauce
- 1 teaspoon dried oregano
- 1 teaspoon chili powder
- 1 teaspoon ground cumin

Directions:

1. For burgers: in a medium pan, heat the oil over medium heat and sauté the onion and garlic for about 5 minutes.
2. With a slotted spoon, transfer the onion mixture into the large bowl.
3. In a food processor, add kale, carrots and parsley and pulse until grated.
4. Transfer the kale mixture into the bowl of onion mixture.
5. In the food processor, add white beans to and pulse until mashed slightly.
6. Transfer the mashed beans into the bowl of kale mixture.
7. For seasoning mixture: in a small mixing bowl, add all ingredients and mix well.
8. Add the cooked quinoa, oats and seasoning mixture in the bowl of kale mixture and mix until well combined.
9. Make 6 equal-sized patties from the mixture.
10. Place the water tray in the bottom of Power XL Smokeless Electric Grill.
11. Place about 2 cups of lukewarm water into the water tray.
12. Place the drip pan over water tray and then arrange the heating element.
13. Now, place the grilling pan over heating element.
14. Plugin the Power XL Smokeless Electric Grill and press the 'Power' button to turn it on.
15. Then press 'Fan" button.
16. Set the temperature settings according to manufacturer's directions.
17. Cover the grill with lid and let it preheat.
18. After preheating, remove the lid and grease the grilling pan.
19. Place the burgers over the grilling pan.
20. Cover with the lid and cook for about 4-5 minutes per side.
21. Serve hot.

Nutrition:

- Info (Per Serving):Calories 489 ;Total Fat 6.4 g ;Saturated Fat 0.9 g   ;Cholesterol 0 mg   ;Sodium 276 mg ;Total Carbs 86.5 g   ;Fiber 24 g ;Sugar 8.4 g   ;Protein 24.1 g

Beef Burgers

Servings: 4
Cooking Time: 8 Minutes

Ingredients:
- 1 pound lean ground beef
- ¼ cup fresh parsley, chopped
- ¼ cup fresh parsley, chopped
- ¼ cup fresh cilantro, chopped
- 1 tablespoon fresh ginger, chopped
- 1 teaspoon ground cumin
- 1 teaspoon ground coriander
- ½ teaspoon ground cinnamon
- Salt and ground black pepper, as required

Directions:
1. In a bowl, add the beef, ¼ cup of parsley, cilantro, ginger, spices, salt and black pepper and mix until well combined.
2. Make 4 equal-sized patties from the mixture.
3. Place the water tray in the bottom of Power XL Smokeless Electric Grill.
4. Place about 2 cups of lukewarm water into the water tray.
5. Place the drip pan over water tray and then arrange the heating element.
6. Now, place the grilling pan over heating element.
7. Plugin the Power XL Smokeless Electric Grill and press the 'Power' button to turn it on.
8. Then press 'Fan" button.
9. Set the temperature settings according to manufacturer's directions.
10. Cover the grill with lid and let it preheat.
11. After preheating, remove the lid and grease the grilling pan.
12. Place the burgers over the grilling pan.
13. Cover with the lid and cook for about for about 3-4 minutes per side or until desired doneness.
14. Serve hot.

Nutrition:
- Info (Per Serving):Calories 220 ;Total Fat 7.3 g ;Saturated Fat 2.7 g ;Cholesterol 101 mg ;Sodium 117 mg ;Total Carbs 1.7 g ;Fiber 0.5 g ;Sugar 0.1 g ;Protein 34.8 g

Italian Panini

Servings: 6

Cooking Time: 5 Minutes

Ingredients:

- 1 loaf rustic Italian bread, sliced
- 4 teaspoons honey mustard
- 12 ounces provolone sliced
- 4 ounces Black Forest ham, thinly sliced
- 4 ounces roast turkey breast, thinly sliced
- 4 ounces Genoa salami, thinly sliced
- 3 tablespoons butter, softened

Directions:

1. Place half of the bread slices on the working surface and brush the top with butter.
2. Divide the honey mustard, provolone, ham, turkey, salami over the bread slices.
3. Set the remaining bread slices on top of the salami.
4. Cut the sandwiches into half diagonally and brush the top with butter.
5. Turn the "Selector" knob to the "Grill Panini" side.
6. Preheat the bottom grill of Cuisine Griddler at 350 degrees F and the upper grill on medium heat.
7. Once it is preheated, place the sandwiches in the grill.
8. Close the griddler's lid and grill the panini for 5 minutes.
9. Serve warm.

Nutrition:

- Info (Per Serving): Calories 424 ;Total Fat 30.2g ;Saturated Fat 16.5g ;Cholesterol 104mg ;Sodium 1449mg ;Total Carbs 8.8g ;Fiber 0.4g ;Sugars 1.2g ;Protein 28.5g

Pork And Veggie Salad

Servings: 1
Cooking Time: 8 Minutes

Ingredients:

- ½ pound Pork Tenderloin
- 1 Lettuce Head
- 1 Tomato, chopped
- 1 Cucumber, chopped
- 1 can Beans, drained
- 1 Carrot, julienned
- 2 tbsp Olive Oil
- 2 tbsp Sour Cream
- 1 tsp Dijon Mustard
- 1 tsp Lemon Juice
- 1 tbsp Honey
- Salt and Pepper, to taste

Directions:

1. Preheat your grill to medium-high.
2. Cut the pork into strips and season with salt and pepper.
3. Coat the grill with cooking spray and arrange the pork onto the bottom plate.
4. Lower the lid so you can cut the cooking time in half and cook for 5 minutes.
5. When done, transfer to a cutting board.
6. If you want to, you can cut the pork into even smaller bite-sized pieces at this point.
7. Add the oil, lemon juice, mustard, honey, sour cream, and some salt and pepper, to a large bowl.
8. Mix well to combine and add the veggies.
9. Toss well to coat.
10. Top the salad with the grilled pork.
11. Enjoy!

Nutrition:

- InfoCalories 240 ;Total Fats 18g ;Carbs 15g ;Protein 20g ;Fiber: 2g

Scrambled Eggs And Cheese

Servings: 2
Cooking Time: 5 Minutes

Ingredients:
- 2 large eggs
- 2 tablespoons milk
- 1/8 teaspoon cayenne pepper
- 1/4 teaspoon salt
- 1 scallion, thinly sliced
- 2 tablespoons cheddar cheese, shredded
- 1 cherry tomato, quartered

Directions:
1. Beat eggs with milk, cayenne pepper, salt, scallion, cheddar, and tomato in a bowl.
2. Open the top lid of the Cuisine Griddler and set the flat plate sides up.
3. Turn the "Selector" knob to the "Grill Panini" side.
4. Preheat the bottom plate of Cuisine Griddler at 350 degrees F and the upper plate on medium heat.
5. Once it is preheated, pour the egg mixture on both plates.
6. Stir and cook the eggs for 5 minutes until set.
7. Serve warm.

Nutrition:
- Info (Per Serving): Calories 117 ;Total Fat 7.7g ;Saturated Fat 3.2g ;Cholesterol 195mg ;Sodium 413mg ;Total Carbs 2.9g ;Fiber 0.6g ;Sugars 2.3g ;Protein 8.7g

Spinach Scrambled Eggs

Servings: 6

Cooking Time: 5 Minutes

Ingredients:

- 2 oz full-fat yogurt
- 1 tablespoon olive oil
- 1 cup spinach, chopped
- 6 large eggs
- ⅓ cup cheddar cheese, shredded

Directions:

1. Beat eggs with olive oil, spinach, cheddar cheese, and yogurt in a bowl.
2. Open the top lid of the Cuisine Griddler and set the flat plate sides up.
3. Turn the "Selector" knob to the "Grill Panini" side.
4. Preheat the bottom plate of Cuisine Griddler at 350 degrees F and the upper plate on medium heat.
5. Once it is preheated, pour the egg mixture on both plates.
6. Stir and cook the eggs for 5 minutes until set.
7. Serve warm.

Nutrition:

- Info (Per Serving): Calories 124 ;Total Fat 9.4g ;Saturated Fat 3.2g ;Cholesterol 193mg ;Sodium 118mg ;Total Carbs 1.7g ;Fiber 0.1g ;Sugars 1.2g ;Protein 8.3g

RECIPES INDEX

Made in United States
Troutdale, OR
06/27/2023

10831179R00060